Wildlife Art

Wildlife Art

60 CONTEMPORARY MASTERS & THEIR WORK

BY JOAN MUYSKENS PURSLEY

First Edition/First Printing

Copyright © 2001 Joan Muyskens Pursley. All rights reserved. No part of the
contents of this book may be reproduced without the written permission
of the publisher.

To purchase additional copies of this book, please contact:
Portfolio Press, 130 Wineow Street, Cumberland, MD 21501. 877-737-1200

Library of Congress Control Number 00-135259

ISBN Number 0-942620-43-7

Project Editor: Krystyna Poray Goddu
Designed by John Vanden-Heuvel Design

Front cover: "Miles to Go" (detail), by Carl Brenders 20⅞ by 31¼
Back cover: "The Gift, Keel-billed," by Gamini Ratnavira, 24 by 40 inches
Pages 2-3: "Run Zebra Run," by Eric Forlee, 24 by 40 inches

Printed and bound in Korea

Contents

Introduction

Wildlife art provides us with windows onto the world's wetlands and wilderness. It takes us on safari to the big game preserves of Africa and introduces us to the exotic denizens of South America's rain forests. It lets us plunge the ocean depths and trek through the mountains and valleys of our national parks without leaving our armchairs. It unearths the still, small creatures in our fields and streams, and shows us the power of the predator, the beauty of the beast, the splendor of the bird on the wing.

Pablo Picasso called art "a lie that makes us realize truth," and when studying wildlife art today, we cannot help but reflect on the validity of that statement. For wildlife art presents lasting images of animals that are fast fading from our lives and our world. It shows us the vitality of beings that are being starved to death because of the destruction of their natural habitats, or being killed en masse for financial gain. By focusing on the beauty of nature, artists like Gamini Ratnavira hope that their paintings will instill "an awareness of nature, its environment and species, and a desire to become involved in conservation efforts." He and many other wildlife artists are active participants in worldwide efforts to preserve the earth's animals. They also give generously to a wide variety of conservation groups. Indeed, it's difficult to think of any other group of artists who work so diligently to preserve the things they paint.

Few people appreciate the natural world more than wildlife artists, most of whom spend as much time "in the field" studying the animals they depict, as they do behind their easels. As Al Agnew explains, "To do justice to any portrayal of wildlife, it is imperative that I get to know the creature and the landscape in which it lives. If one has a basic understanding of an animal and has seen and studied its habitat, ideas for paintings of that animal are unlimited." Of course, as John Seerey-Lester points out, animals in their natural habitat "do not pose for you." Getting to know them can take years of research and observation.

Some artists, such as Robert Deurloo and Terry Redlin, live in areas of abundant wildlife, but for many, research means extensive and often expensive travel. It can also mean risk, as they attempt to get up close and personal with their subjects. "When working with dangerous game, a mistake can and often is fatal," says Gary Swanson. "I have, however, made them. I choose not to divulge just how ignorant I have been, but I will say this: I have been in serious trouble with all five of Africa's 'Big 5' [cape buffalo, elephant, rhino, lion and leopard]—and all in one day."

He's far from the only artist to have run-ins with wildlife, and it can happen wherever one finds big animals. "While filming and working on a buffalo ranch, I was charged twice by cows," Lee Cable admits. "The first time, the cow's shoulder actually made contact with my hip as she charged by." The second time around, the artist was a bit faster on his feet.

"California Hare" is from John James Audubon's *The Viviparous Quadrupeds of North America*. (Photo: Sepp Seitz)

changed me forever."

Bruce Miller thought he was playing it safe when he needed to study grizzlies. He opted to photograph a large, pen-raised, fenced-in female grizzly, rather than head into the hills. His trouble began when the bear's owner insisted he get inside the fence to shoot his photos. "After about 15 to 20 minutes, the grizzly noticed me," Miller says. "She walked over, put one foot on each of my feet and stuck her head right in my crotch; then she wanted to wrestle. At that point, I yelled for the owner," he admits, "and slowly left the pen."

Patti Wilson wasn't even looking for wildlife when she had a close encounter with a bear. "On one of our many camping trips in the Sierra Nevada mountains," she says, "a big brown bear came into our campsite while we were there and tore apart our camp table. As we tried to scare him off, he stood up. The size of him scared us so much that we couldn't sleep for the next two nights." Surprisingly, the artist and her husband, Don, continue to camp at that same site every year.

The Legacy of John James Audubon

Trevor Swanson, Gary Swanson's son, also had a run-in with a buffalo—this one a cape buffalo that he encountered in Africa. Swanson was in Botswana's Okavango delta region, an area of thick jungles and grasslands, with a group scouting for leopards and cape buffalo. They found signs of both, and then came upon some buffalo. "After watching the buffalo," he says, "we decided to walk back to camp, instead of taking the mokoros [dugout canoes]. We were crossing near some dense jungle when a buffalo that we must have cut off from the herd came charging out of the brush straight toward us. It came at me with its head down, and I only had time to turn my back a little when I was slammed up into the air by the curve of her horns. I remember thinking of all the terrible stories one hears of buffalo killing more people than lions, so when I hit the ground I was ready for anything. Fortunately, the buffalo just ran on to join the rest of the herd, but it

One of the best-known wildlife artists of the past, John James Audubon had several things in common with today's wildlife artists. The first was a passion for nature, which stemmed from his childhood spent exploring the woods and fields around his home, studying and sketching the birds he found in them. Then there was his desire to depict the birds in lifelike poses, rather than as ornithological studies. Finally, there was his recognition of the importance of field work—that without a true understanding of his subject, he was unable to accurately depict it.

The son of a French naval captain, Audubon was born in 1785, in Aux Cayes, Santo Domingo (now Haiti), raised in France, then sent to work on his father's Pennsylvania plantation when he was 18. There, he discovered a whole new world of birds, so different from those of his childhood; his fascination with them eventually led to a determination to paint all the birds found in North America.

Due in large part to the support of his wife, Lucy Bakewell, Audubon was able to travel extensively, searching for new species to observe and paint. He spent about 17 years completing the artwork for *The Birds of America*. The elephant folio engravings for this book were made in England between 1826 and 1838 by William H. Lizars and Robert Havell, Jr.; the complete set, sold by subscription, comprises 435 plates featuring 1,065 life-size birds. Small, hand-colored lithographs of Audubon's birds were later published. Also, after Audubon's death, his younger son, John Woodhouse Audubon, had some of *The Birds of America* elephant folios reproduced by chromolithography.

After completing the artwork for his book on birds, Audubon began work on a similar, large-folio book featuring North American mammals. John Bachman, a Lutheran minister in Charleston, South Carolina, assisted Audubon on this project; Bachman was a long-time friend of Audubon, and his daughters were married to Audubon's sons. After creating about half the artwork for the book, *The Quadrupeds of North America*, Audubon had a stroke and was unable to do any additional artwork. His younger son, John Woodhouse, completed the drawings his father had started and did all the remaining drawings, almost half of them, himself. Audubon's elder son, Victor, painted most of the backgrounds. Bachman wrote the text for the book, assisted by Victor and using, in part, notes that Audubon and his younger son had taken on their many field trips.

With the publication of *The Birds of America*, Audubon became well known in Europe and the United States. He wrote a text to accompany his bird engravings—it describes the habits of the birds he drew, plus tells about life in America during the 1820s and '30s—and he wrote for scientific journals. The original elephant folios of his bird illustrations have been popular since they were first published. On March 10, 2000, at Christie's New York auction house, one of the original, four-volume subscriber sets of *The Birds in America* was hammered down for $8,802,500, setting a world-record price realized for a printed book. (The previous record, according to Francis Wahlgren, head of Christie's New York Book & Manuscript Department, was $7.6 million, paid for Chaucer's *The Canterbury Tales*, sold at Christie's London in July of 1998.) Individual plates from the book may bring as much as $100,000 to $150,000 at auction.

The National Audubon Society

When Audubon was traveling along the Eastern Seaboard, up and down the Mississippi River, and through the American West observing wildlife, it was still abundant. But that was not the case by the end of

Jay Norwood ("Ding") Darling's artwork is featured on this first (1934-35) Federal Duck Stamp.

the 19th century. As the population grew, the prairies, forests, plains and wetlands necessary for the survival of wildlife were being lost to urban sprawl. Adding to the problem was the industrial pollution of lakes, rivers and streams. Uncontrolled hunting took its toll, but much worse was the commercial killing of literally millions of birds and animals for their feathers and meat. By the early 1900s, some species, such as the passenger pigeon, Carolina parakeet and great auk, were extinct and the future of others was threatened.

Concerned about the massive slaughter of birds, George Bird Grinnell, the editor of *Forest and Stream* magazine, organized a preservation society in 1886. He named it the Audubon Society, for John James Audubon, and urged his readers to join. The response of his readership was impressive; in just three months, Grinnell's society had more than 38,000 members. Unfortunately, that success was its downfall; Grinnell didn't have the staff or organizational skills to cope with the large membership, and ended up disbanding the society in 1888.

Fortunately, the passion for preservation that Grinnell sparked in so many survived the original Audubon Society. In 1896, the Massachusetts Audubon Society was formed by a group of concerned women, who refused to purchase hats and clothing decorated with feathers. They also began a letter-writing campaign to newspapers and government officials to call attention to the slaughter of whole species of birds. Other states formed similar organizations, and by 1899, there were 17 state Audubon Societies. That same year, ornithologist Frank Chapman's first issue of *Bird Lore* magazine was published by the American Museum of Natural History, located in New York City. In 1900, Chapman organized the first Christmas Bird Count—a national event that continues to be held annually.

Introduction

In 1901, the National Committee of the Audubon Societies was formed; four years later, it was incorporated into the National Association of Audubon Societies for the Protection of Wild Birds and Animals. Among its early political successes were the 1910 passage of the New York State Audubon Plumage Law, which banned the sale of plumes of all native birds in the state, and the 1918 passage of the Federal Migratory Bird Treaty Act. The group also began purchasing land to form wildlife sanctuaries for animals as well as birds; its largest, acquired in 1924, is the Paul J. Rainey Sanctuary, a 26,000-acre area in Louisiana.

Today, the National Audubon Society—the name it adopted in 1940—has more than 500 chapters and 550,000 members. Its national headquarters are located in a century-old building at 700 Broadway, New York City. The organization also has 100 Audubon Sanctuaries and nature centers nationwide, and it employs approximately 300 people, including scientists, sanctuary managers, regional and state directors, educators and lobbyists.

The National Audubon Society continues to work for increased public awareness of wildlife issues and for the passage of laws that will preserve wildlife and its

The 2000-01 Federal Duck Stamp features this painting of a mottled duck by Adam Grimm—the youngest artist to win the contest. It has been published by Steiner Prints, San Francisco, California, in four editions, each including one of the stamps.

environment. Its Junior Audubon club, founded in 1910, educates children about birds and the importance of their protection. For adults, it publishes *Audubon Magazine*, an outgrowth of Chapman's *Bird Lore*, which the Society purchased from the American Museum of Natural History in 1935. It also sponsors an Audubon Adventures program for children and summer ecology camps for adults.

As it enters the 21st century, the Audubon Society has defined eight "high-priority campaigns and key legislative programs." They are: preserving wetlands; lobbying to reauthorize the Endangered Species Act; promoting a responsible United States population policy; preserving America's endangered forests; protecting and promoting growth of America's National Wildlife Refuges; conserving marine wildlife through the Living Oceans program; the restoration of water flows to enhance wildlife of the Platte River system; and protecting corridors for migratory birds through the Partners in Flight program.

Duck Stamps

Back in the 1920s, a diverse group of conservationists, hunters and public officials concerned particularly about the decreasing numbers of American waterfowl worked together to pass the Migratory Bird Conservation Act of 1929. It authorized the Department of Agriculture to acquire and maintain wetlands necessary for the survival of ducks, geese, swans and other water birds. What the act didn't do, however, was provide funds for this important conservation work. Generally credited with solving this problem is Jay Norwood ("Ding") Darling. An avid hunter, conservationist and Pulitzer-prize-winning political cartoonist, Darling drew attention to the destruction of waterfowl and its habitat through his illustrations for *The Des Moines Register.*

In 1934, President Franklin D. Roosevelt asked Darling to head up the Bureau of Biological Survey, which later became the United States Fish and Wildlife Service. Darling developed a simple program that required all waterfowl hunters age 16 and over to buy a stamp and affix it to their license. The funds raised from the sale of the stamp would then be used to purchase and preserve United States wetlands. This program became official on March 16, 1934, when Congress passed the Migratory Bird Hunting Stamp Act and President Roosevelt signed it.

The first of what became known as the "Federal Duck Stamp" was designed by Darling, at the request of President Roosevelt; priced at just $1, it was introduced in August of 1934 and was purchased by some 635,000 hunters. Today, federal duck stamps sell for $15 each and are purchased by approximately 1.5 million people, a combination of hunters and stamp collectors. More than $500 million has been raised through sales of the stamps—money that has been used to preserve close to 4.5 million acres of waterfowl habitat located throughout the United States.

From 1935 to 1949, wildlife artists were invited to design the duck stamps. In 1949, however, the U.S. Fish and Wildlife Service decided to hold an annual contest to select the duck stamp image—a contest that continues to be held today. The Federal Duck Stamp contest is open to all United States artists, who are allowed use any medium for their design. The winning artwork is selected by a panel of art, waterfowl and philatelic experts appointed by the Secretary of the Interior. The first year, 65 artists submitted designs for

By Adele Earnshaw, this painting of paradise shelducks is featured on the 1994 First of Nation New Zealand Game Bird Habitat Stamp. Like the conservation stamp programs of many countries, New Zealand's is modeled on that of the United States. Purchase of the stamp is mandatory to validate a hunting license, and revenue from the program is used to purchase, protect, improve and maintain game bird habitat.

the stamp. By the early 1980s, more than 2,000 artists were participating in the contest. That number has since dropped, in part because there is now a $100 fee for each entry, which has discouraged some amateurs from participating. There is no monetary prize for the winner, but there is national recognition, as Adam Grimm discovered when he won the 1999 contest.

The youngest artist to ever win a Federal Duck Stamp competition, Grimm was a 21-year-old college student when his painting of a drake mottled duck won the contest (the image appears on the 2000-01 stamp). "My teachers at Columbus College of Art & Design really discouraged realism and wildlife as a subject," he says. They would look at his work, and ask him what his artistic goals were. "I'd tell them that I hoped to win

the Federal Duck Stamp competition," Grimm says, "but they didn't know what I was talking about." That changed when Grimm won. "All these reporters were calling the school looking for me, and calling my professors wanting quotes." While he's too nice a guy to say it, you know how great he must have felt to be getting so much national attention for a realistic painting of ducks—just the kind of painting that his professors so looked down upon.

Another advantage of winning the Federal Duck Stamp contest is that artists are permitted to sell prints of their winning design—prints that became hot collectibles. "I got a studio with the money from the sale of the print of my winning artwork," says Nancy Howe; the first woman to win the competition, her artwork graces the 1991-92 stamp. Also, she notes, "winning the competition catapulted me into shows and gave me name recognition that otherwise would have taken me five or ten years to attain."

There has been an ebbing of interest in the Duck Stamp prints over the past decade or so, in part because there are now numerous other wildlife art contests. Each of the 50 states, for instance, now has its own Duck Stamp program. (Hawaii was the last state to jump onto this fund-raising bandwagon with its 1996-97 stamp and print.) So do many foreign countries. Also, the availability of prints featuring top artists' work has increased significantly over the past two decades. Still, winning the Federal Duck Stamp Contest remains a top honor for wildlife artists, and as Robert Steiner, whose art was selected for the 1998-99 Federal Duck Stamp, says, "The number of artists entering the competition may be decreasing, but the quality of the entries is better than ever." The top 20 entries in each year's contest are exhibited throughout the year at museums, art shows and festivals around the country, bringing attention to the genre as well as to individual artists.

Also generating interest in wildlife art is the Federal Junior Duck Stamp Conservation and Design Program. It was begun in 1989-90 to encourage conservation through the arts; since 1994, money raised from the sale of the Junior Duck Stamps is funneled back to schools participating in the program, through awards and scholarships given to teachers and students. The contest is open to kindergarten through high school students, who compete first on the state level. The Best of Show design from each state is then entered into the national contest. Adam Grimm, who had entered two of the Junior Duck Stamp Contests during his high school years, now enjoys visiting schools and sharing his experience with budding artists. He encourages youngsters to enter the contest, and he gives them tips on how to create winning paintings.

Although the Federal Duck Stamp prints may not be as hot today as they were a decade or two ago, they remain popular with collectors, as do the stamps. According to the U.S. Fish and Wildlife Service, values of the Federal Duck Stamps, especially the early ones, have increased significantly. The pre-1941 stamps are the rarest and most valuable, because stamps issued before 1941 were destroyed the following year. Today, the U.S. Fish and Wildlife Service and the U.S. Postal Service are permitted to sell each year's stamp for a period of three years.

In 1992, a group of duck stamp collectors banded together and formed the National Duck Stamp Collectors Society (PO Box 43, Harleysville, PA 19438). The organization currently has about 400 members. Its annual membership dues are $20, and include a subscription to a quarterly newsletter, titled *Duck Tracks*.

Many Groups, Common Goals

The Federal Duck Stamp program isn't alone in raising money for waterfowl and wetlands conservation. Ducks Unlimited has also made a significant difference in the preservation of North America's birds. Founded in 1936 by Joseph Knapp, and incorporated the following year, its initial goal was to raise money in the United States for waterfowl conservation in Canada, where most of the North American waterfowl breed.

Today, the organization's mission is "to fulfill the annual life-cycle needs of North American waterfowl by protecting, enhancing, restoring and managing important wetlands and associated uplands." To date, it has raised more than $1.4 billion, which has been used for the conservation of more than nine million acres of wildlife habitat, not just in Canada, but also in the United States and Mexico. Many wildlife artists donate original paintings and prints to Ducks Unlimited, for use as fund-raisers.

Another organization that many artists support is the World Wildlife Fund (WWF). Founded in 1961 by a small group of conservationists—including ornithologist Max Nicholson, then Director General of Britain's Nature Conservancy, and ornithologist Peter Scott, a vice-president of The World Conservation Union—it serves as a fund-raising agency for wildlife conservation projects around the world.

WWF gives money to small and large projects, and works with both private and government groups. One of its early grants, for instance, paid for a road grader and rotary mower for Kenya's Masai Mara Game Reserve. On a larger scale, in 1969 WWF worked with the Spanish government to purchase a section of the Guadalquivir Delta marshes and establish the Coto Donana National Park, an important wetland area. It has

worked with the Chinese Ministry of Forestry on a giant panda management plan. Also, it has helped preserve the lechwes in Zambia's Kafue Flats through a program that trained local people as wildlife scouts; due in large part to this program, the lechwe population has increased enough for the country to allow limited hunting of lechwes. Under the current program, trophy hunters pay a fee to hunt the animal, with the money used for community development and wildlife management.

"There are so many animals out there that are in trouble," says Linda Thompson, "but for every endangered animal, there seems to be an organization that is helping to save it, and an artist who is willing to donate to the cause. I've even done paintings of the mountain gorilla for an organization in Africa that is trying to save them. Even though I paint things that live in the water, I'll donate art to help other endangered species if I can."

Among the other organizations supported by wildlife artists featured in the pages of this book are the Ruffed Grouse Society, Quail Unlimited, Rocky Mountain Elk Foundation and the National Wild Turkey Federation. The goal of the Ruffed Grouse Society, founded in 1961 in Monterey, Virginia, is to improve woodland habitat for ruffed grouse, the American woodcock and other forest wildlife. It provides technical and financial assistance to groups managing public lands, and presents seminars on forest management and conservation techniques for private owners of forested areas. It has approximately 23,000 members and 130 chapters in the United States and Canada.

Quail Unlimited, established in 1981 to battle the problem of dwindling quail and wildlife habitat, has more than 400 chapters in the United States. It works with the U.S. Forest Service to increase food, cover and water for wild quail and other upland game. It encourages and, at times, pays farmers to leave grain in their fields to serve as winter food for wildlife. It also encourages farmers to leave existing tree rows on their property by providing them with root plows—tools that help farmers produce better crops next to trees. Educating Americans about the importance of conservation is also important to Quail Unlimited, which publishes newsletters and sponsors seminars and a camp for youth. Youth programs stress conservation of our natural, renewable resources; they also provide information on safe gun handling, firearm maintenance and hunter ethics.

A relative newcomer to the conservation scene, The Rocky Mountain Elk Foundation was formed in 1984 by four Montana hunters. Headquartered in Missoula, Montana, it has a simple mission: "to ensure the future of elk, other wildlife and their habitat." Its projects include increasing forage on elks' grazing lands, installing water catchment basins in arid areas and moving elk into areas with suitable habitat but low populations. The Rocky Mountain Elk Foundation also funds research projects and educational programs, in an effort to ensure the survival of elk for future generations.

The National Wild Turkey Federation has proven how effective conservation efforts can be when a group of people work together. When it was founded in 1973, there were 1.3 million wild turkeys in the United States. Today, according to the 215,000-member organization, there are some 5 million. Headquartered in Edgefield, South Carolina, this organization has raised and spent $120 million on conservation and education programs that benefit the preservation of wild turkeys in the United States, Canada and Mexico.

Leigh Yawkey Woodson Art Museum

While artists help promote conservation, a small museum in Wausau, Wisconsin, does a lot to promote wildlife art. It's the Leigh Yawkey Woodson Art Museum, founded in 1976. Leigh Yawkey Woodson's three daughters—Nancy Woodson Spire, Alice Woodson Forester and Margaret Woodson Fisher—were instrumental in founding the museum as a memorial to their mother. Leigh Yawkey Woodson was a lover of wildlife; among her prized possessions was a collection of life-size porcelain birds by English sculptress Dorothy Doughty. These porcelains are part of the museum's permanent collection.

To mark the museum's grand opening in the fall of 1976, Alice Woodson Forester and her husband, John, suggested that Wisconsin wildlife painter Owen J. Gromme (1896-1991) be asked to curate a temporary exhibit featuring avian art. The exhibition was titled "Birds of the Lakes, Fields and Forests," and was so successful that it became an annual fall event. Now titled "Birds in Art," it regularly features about 115 artworks. Each year the museum honors one artist with the title of Master Wildlife Artist, and includes about a dozen of that artist's work in the exhibition. All past Master Wildlife Artists are invited to submit one work to each annual exhibit; the winning paintings for the Federal Duck Stamp and the Wisconsin Duck Stamp also are shown. The other pieces featured are selected by a jury from entered artworks. Generally, about 1,000 artworks by 600 different artists are submitted; about 90 of them get selected for display.

Since 1979, traveling "Birds in Art" exhibits have visited major American museums, such as the Smithsonian National Collection of Fine Arts in Washington, D.C., and Chicago's Field Museum of Natural History, thus exposing millions of Americans to top wildlife art. Also, selected works from exhibits have toured China and been displayed at the Royal Scottish Academy in Edinburgh and the British Museum of Natural History in London.

Looking to the Future

Despite the far-flung attention that the Leigh Yawkey Woodson Art Museum's "Birds in Art" exhibitions have brought to wildlife art, the fact remains that exhibits of wildlife art in this country are generally limited to natural history museums. Unfortunately, the genre is simply not considered "fine art" by curators of major American art museums.

"Wildlife art has been accepted in every single culture through the centuries, except ours," says Robert Bateman. "You find paintings of animals in the tombs of ancient Egypt, in early Greek murals, in centuries-old Chinese and Japanese art. But for some reason, with the rise of the Christian church as the dominant power in Western culture, nature was put in a subservient place. Wild animals were seen as a threat. If they did appear in art, they were at the end of a spear or hanging by their legs with a bunch of grapes, ready for the table." Domestic animals, Bateman notes, were acceptable artistic subjects, and were painted by everyone from Reubens through Picasso, but wild animals—viewed eye-to-eye with respect—simply aren't to be found in the mainstream of Western art.

Today's wildlife artists are hoping to change that. But in order to succeed, Greg Beecham says, "wildlife art has to take a step forward, a step up from being a naturalist's rendering of an animal with a few plants around it, to really making artistic statements." Beecham regrets that so much wildlife art is simply portraits of animals. "Very little of it evokes any kind of emotion, any kind of mood; very little says anything artistically. If we want to progress as a genre, if we want to build, then we have to pursue *art* within the context of the wildlife genre."

Beecham's sentiments are echoed by a number of the artists featured on the following pages. Most, however, are also optimistic about the future of wildlife art and the growing attention it is getting, if not from major art museums, at least from major auction houses. In 1994, Christie's London South Kensington auction house staged an impressive sale of contemporary wildlife art. So popular was the auction that Christie's now holds not one, but two wildlife art auctions every year—one in May and the other in November. While the contemporary artworks aren't being hammered down for hundreds of thousands of dollars, they are commanding active bidding and healthy prices, and the sales have a growing audience.

"I think as long as people love the natural world, there is a future for wildlife art—perhaps a brighter future as the open spaces and species of this world disappear. Sadly, I think this will make wildlife art more important," says Adele Earnshaw. "I strongly feel that the wildlife art of the last and coming centuries will, in time, become as important as the work of the Impressionists, because we are recording a disappearing world."

Awesome records of this disappearing world appear on the following pages of this book—paintings and sculptures by 60 of today's top wildlife artists. Many of these artists have had their work included in the Leigh Yawkey Woodson Art Museum's prestigious "Birds in Art" exhibitions; many also have had their work featured on conservation stamps. All of them have examples of their artworks reproduced in affordable limited editions.

The Artists

Al Agnew

I believe a wildlife artist has a duty and obligation to present the natural world with authenticity, accuracy and sensitivity," says Al Agnew. "I want my creatures to be anatomically and behaviorally correct. However, I also want to convey my own sense of awe and appreciation for the wild creatures and wild places, and to inspire viewers to cherish nature as I do."

Agnew's love of nature and passion for art stem from his childhood. Born in Desloge, Missouri, in 1952, he spent his early years roaming the hills and dales of Missouri's Ozarks, picking up turtles, snakes and other critters, then taking them home to study and draw. His roaming days were interrupted by college (he earned a B.S. in education from Southeast Missouri State University) and seven years of teaching art. However, Agnew continues to live in the Ozarks, and since he began painting full-time in 1983, he's once again searching for subjects in the great outdoors.

"I believe there is no substitute for becoming personally familiar with the animals and their habitat. I spend a lot of time visiting wild places all over North America as well as Africa, and I also study animals in zoos, wildlife parks and other captive situations. I generally do extensive field sketches and color studies, make field notes, and also rely on my own photography," the artist says. Visits to zoos are helpful, but, Agnew stresses, they are never a substitute for observing wildlife in its natural habitat. "Only familiarity with an animal in the wild can tell you what the similarities and differences with captive animals are," he asserts.

The artist describes his style as "realistic and detailed," but notes that he hopes his paintings are about more than fine detail. "I not only want to place the viewer in the painting, but also to elicit a feeling of having been there before." He succeeds in doing this because of his familiarity with the animals' environments and the artistic attention he gives not just to the animals, but also to his paintings' backgrounds.

While Agnew is "fascinated by all predators, from freshwater game fish to eagles to wolves," he is an ardent conservationist. His artworks have helped raise millions of dollars for such organizations as Ducks Unlimited, the Sierra Club and the Black Bass Foundation. He was the official artist for the National Park Service Yellowstone

"Catching the Sunset" is 30 inches wide by 20 inches high. "Laying About," opposite page, is 9 inches wide by 12 inches high. Predators appear in a number of Agnew's paintings, as the artist finds their social interactions and predator-prey relationships offer endless possibilities for paintings.

Wolf Recovery Project; he has designed eleven state hunting and fishing stamps; and he was selected to create the 1993 National Wild Turkey Federation Stamp Print.

Agnew's artwork has been featured in a number of museum exhibitions, including the Leigh Yawkey Woodson Art Museum's "Birds in Art" and "Animals, The Artist View" exhibits, and the Society of Animal Artists' "Art and the Animal" annual show. His paintings have also appeared in national magazines, including *Outdoor Life, Field & Stream* and *Wildlife Art News.* His medium of choice is chromacolour acrylics, but he also uses watercolors. Prices for his original paintings begin around $2,000 and go up to $35,000; prints of his work, published by Hadley House, Bloomington, Minnesota, are available for considerably less.

"The Road Less Traveled," 30 inches wide by 20 inches high, has been published by Hadley House in a limited edition of 750 prints.

John Banovich

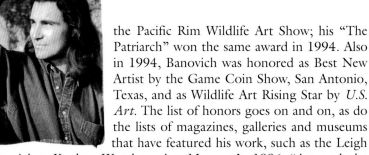

I find myself drawn to larger species, particularly predators—large cats, bears, wolves," says John Banovich. "I paint global wildlife, and spend about 20 to 25 percent of my time in the field. That includes research trips throughout North America, Africa, Europe. I'm about to go to Uganda to study mountain gorillas, then to Serengeti and the Morogoro crater in Tanzania." Banovich has a special love for Africa and its wildlife, and he shares that love through his art, and through collector and artist safaris. The collector safaris "grew out of people wanting to see how a painting is birthed, how the idea originates. So this is a great opportunity not only for me to share my art, but also to share my vision of things. I've been on almost 20 safaris. I've got a lot of contacts. I know a lot of places to go to get the best experience," he says.

Born in Butte, Montana, in 1964, Banovich studied art and zoology at the University of Montana. He then attended the Art Institute of Seattle, where he earned a

the Pacific Rim Wildlife Art Show; his "The Patriarch" won the same award in 1994. Also in 1994, Banovich was honored as Best New Artist by the Game Coin Show, San Antonio, Texas, and as Wildlife Art Rising Star by *U.S. Art*. The list of honors goes on and on, as do the lists of magazines, galleries and museums that have featured his work, such as the Leigh Yawkey Woodson Art Museum's 1996 "Art and the Animal" and 1997 "Birds in Art" exhibitions.

Banovich's impressive career is due not only to his talent, but also to his insistence that each and every one of his paintings tells a story and evokes an emotional response. "In wildlife art, there's so much good technical skill, where people are able to capture the fur, the feathers, and that's great stuff. But for me," says Banovich, "an artist must communicate an emotion, a feeling. Forget that the subject happens to be wildlife. Forget that it happens to be realism. That's totally irrelevant. That makes no difference whatsoever from an artist's standpoint. A painting has to be a great piece of art. It has to be something that will move you. You may not like the subject. You may not relate to it. You may think its disgusting—like if I do a kill scene or something. But if I've communicated something visceral, that's the important thing."

In addition to being passionate about his art, Banovich feels strongly about wildlife preservation, to which he takes a "hands-on" approach.

"Winter Shadows" is 48⅛ inches wide by 20⅛ inches high. "Great White," opposite page, is 50 inches wide by 60 inches high. John Banovich describes his style as "somewhat impressionistic. It's slightly loose," he says, "but it reads as realism. I put a lot of breathing space between my strokes. I let a lot of underpainting show through. I try to show as much as I can with the least amount of stroke or effort with paint," he explains.

degree in visual communications. He made Seattle his home until recently, when he moved back to Montana, settling near Livingston and Yellowstone National Park.

He's been painting full-time since 1993, the year his "In the Heat of the Day" won the Best of Show award at

An example of this is the Botetie River Project in Botswana. "The river dried up about ten years ago, and the animals couldn't migrate because fences were put up to keep the cattle and wild animals separate. So we drilled a bore hole and put in a well and camp, and hired local people to manage it. Now the animals are no longer dying from thirst and starvation. This is the kind of project I love to do—hands-on, ground-level projects, with all the money going right to the source," he says.

Banovich's originals sell for as much as $48,000. Prints of his paintings are published by Mill Pond Press, Venice, Florida.

John Banovich's "Going for the Gold," an original oil on canvas, is 24 inches wide by 36 inches high. His "Misty Encounter," right, is 62 inches wide by 48½ inches high. (Photos: Richard Nicol)

Robert Bateman

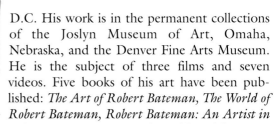

No artist has influenced the style of American wildlife art more than Robert Bateman. A Canadian—Bateman was born in Toronto, in 1930—he began painting nature in his youth, experimenting with many styles, from representational to impressionism, cubism and abstract expressionism. He attended the University of Toronto, where he earned a degree in geography, and then taught high school for 20 years, two of which were in Nigeria. By the time he was 30, Bateman was "a landscape painter who did abstracts and was an avid naturalist at the same time," he says.

What Bateman calls his "epiphany" came in the early 1960s, when he saw Andrew Wyeth's work at a Buffalo, New York, gallery. "I suddenly saw that realism was the only true way to portray nature," says the artist, who began painting animals in a full landscape treated somewhat photographically. The sheer beauty of Bateman's work, and his success, have inspired a lot of artists, many of whom have embraced his style.

Bateman, who has been painting full-time since 1976, has had many one-man shows at major American museums, such as the Smithsonian Institution in Washington,

D.C. His work is in the permanent collections of the Joslyn Museum of Art, Omaha, Nebraska, and the Denver Fine Arts Museum. He is the subject of three films and seven videos. Five books of his art have been published: *The Art of Robert Bateman, The World of Robert Bateman, Robert Bateman: An Artist in Nature, Robert Bateman: Natural Worlds* and his most recent, *Safari,* an illustrated book of African animals geared to young readers. He's been the subject of magazine articles too numerous to mention.

The Leigh Yawkey Woodson Art Museum honored Bateman as its Master Wildlife Artist at the 1982 "Birds in Art" exhibition. He was made an Officer of the Order of Canada, his country's highest civilian award. He has a Golden Plate award from the American Academy of Achievement, and the National Audubon Society has named him one of the 20th Century's Champions of Conservation. Bateman has been an active conservation-

"Sudden Move—Siberian Tiger" has been published by Mill Pond Press on paper and canvas; both are 32½ inches wide by 16¼ inches high. The print on paper is limited to a signed and numbered edition of 2,500, plus 76 artist proofs; the canvas is limited to an edition of 180, plus 11 artist proofs.

"By the River," an acrylic on canvas, is 72 inches wide by 48 inches high. Bateman is intimate with the animals of Africa; he taught school in Nigeria for two years, and has visited the continent more than two dozen times over a period of 40-plus years. "Hindu Temple—Tiger," right, is 42 inches wide by 24 inches high. Limited-edition prints of Bateman's paintings are published by Mill Pond Press.

ist since the early 1960s; his original paintings and his prints, published by Mill Pond Press, Venice, Florida, have raised millions of dollars for various preservation causes.

During his long career, Bateman has traveled the world. He made the first of his many trips to Africa in 1957. "Every time I've gone back," he says, "I've had better luck than before—on my last trip, I saw more than 150 lions, 28 cheetahs, 11 leopards—but I can see the handwriting on the wall with the human population rising and corruption rising. It's a worrisome situation....When you fly over the country, you can see the rate at which the forests are being cut down. This is not in the parks, but on the borders of the parks, the forest is being cut down and little shambas, little farms are being built, covering everything."

About the future of wildlife art, Bateman says, "It's here to stay, because wildlife appreciation is continuing to rise. It is never going to subside, because as each year goes by, wildlife is going to be more and more precious, as more and more things become extinct, and we realize that it's vulnerable."

Robert Bateman's art reflects his broad commitment to ecology and preservation. Shown here is his "Ocean Rhapsody," a 96-inch-wide by 48-inch-high acrylic on canvas.

Greg Beecham

"When I was in fifth or sixth grade, my dad sat me down and taught me to draw," says Greg Beecham, the son of illustrator and wildlife artist Tom Beecham. "I learned at that time how to draw photographically. I could take any picture you'd give to me and make an exact copy of it." Since his four sisters and brother were also artistic, this talent didn't seem all that remarkable to young Beecham. He enjoyed drawing, but didn't envision following in his father's footsteps.

Three days after graduating from high school, Beecham left Goshen, New York, where he was born in 1954, and joined the navy. He served on the USS *John S. McCain*, a guided-missile destroyer, and later as a hospital corpsman. By the time he got out of the service, he knew he wanted to be an artist. He went to Southern Oregon State College, where he studied art and history, and "met my wife. In 1978, she graduated, so I quite college. We went back to New York for the summer, and I studied art full-time with my dad."

Having his father for a teacher was anything but a snap, though. "I would work for a week, then take everything I'd done to dad. He would tear it to pieces, and I'd go back all depressed and do it over again. I did that all summer," says Beecham. It was great training, but even-tually Beecham realized he had to develop a style of his own. "People would say, 'Oh, your work looks just like your father's, but it's not as good,'" he says with a laugh. "So I went in different directions in terms of composition, in terms of color usage, of brush work."

At summer's end, Beecham and his wife moved to the Pacific Northwest, where he did commercial illustrations to pay the bills, and painted animals and their habitat because he finds "the abstract patterns in both landscapes and animals are too fascinating to ignore." Beecham refers to his work as "accessible abstractions." Painting primarily with oils on linen, he uses an impasto technique. "I like a lot of texture. I think texture has a lot to say in terms of where I'm going with my art," he notes.

"I have no great message for my art. For me, the abstract design elements are more important than saying 'here's a moose.' I'm interested in making an artistic

"Step Into the Light," 33 inches wide by 16 inches high, has been published by The Greenwich Workshop in a signed and numbered edition of 550. "Except for my plein air work, all of my landscapes have animals in them," says Greg Beecham, explaining: "I don't think as a typical landscape artist. I think in terms of focal point, of the eye moving in and around the animal and out into a scene. A landscapist doesn't necessarily think that way. I'm pretty much a wildlife artist."

"Mystic Warrior," 18½ inches wide by 13¾ inches high, is a good example of Beecham's painterly technique and ability to evoke emotions with mood and atmosphere. It has been published in a signed and numbered edition of 550. "Bustin' Through," left, is 26 inches wide by 20⅛ inches high; it has been published by The Greenwich Workshop in a signed and numbered edition of 750.

Dubois, Wyoming, a town of 900 located in what Beecham considers some of the most beautiful country in the world. "We love to get up into the high country on our horses and see wilderness and the animals and go fishing," he says. Another love: plein air painting. "I do that as often as I can, because it obviously is of great help to the studio work, and it sells, too."

composition using landscape and animals as my motif. Yes, I love the animals, but what I love about them is how artistic they are. So that's my direction—creating artistic images that say something, that evoke emotions with mood and atmosphere as well as texture, brushwork and abstract design."

The artist, his wife and their two children now live in

Beecham's paintings have been exhibited in Beijing, China's Museum of Natural History, and are in the permanent collections of the Leigh Yawkey Woodson Art Museum, Wausau, Wisconsin, and the Clymer Museum, Ellensburg, Washington. His work appears on several series of collector plates, and prints of his paintings are published by The Greenwich Workshop.

Ted Blaylock

Art, for me, is something I would be doing on Saturdays and Sundays for nothing but pleasure—if I wasn't making my living from painting," says Ted Blaylock. "Few people can go through life never feeling like they have a job; the creative process of art is all consuming—the mind sends you on field trips at the least expected moments."

Born in Perryville, Missouri, in 1940, Blaylock has been a professional painter for more than 35 years. During that time, his art has garnered many first place and Best of Show awards. It has been included in the Leigh Yawkey Woodson Museum's "Birds in Art" exhibition, and selected for the Arizona Lifetime Trout Stamp and the 1990-91 Arizona Duck Stamp. He was inducted into the Arizona Outdoor Hall of Fame in 1998, and that same year was honored as Wildlife for Tomorrow's Artist of the Year.

Blaylock, who has had little formal art training—just one semester of study at St. Louis University and a few classes at Scottsdale Artist School—says that "as a child, I was given the talent to sketch. It was fun, but the recognition that I had a gift was never important. My grade school and high school teachers reinforced my love for the arts, so as a child I knew I wanted to be an artist."

His interest in wildlife was stimulated by a teacher at his church, who took him into the country for field studies. "I found I could not go too long in the city without an outing to the woods and lakes," says Blaylock, who became an avid birdwatcher and student of woodland lore.

Today, he continues to make field trips, including many to Alaska, and to enjoy close encounters with nature. "On one trip to photograph bull elk, I was calling one in with a mewing cow call. I was laying in the grass, in camouflage clothing, when all of a sudden, I looked up and saw a blur coming toward me." The blur was a goshawk, which got about five feet from his eyes before turning aside. "It was diving at me, thinking the noise I was making was coming from some small animal," says the artist with a laugh.

In addition to painting elk and other North American animals and birds, Blaylock paints rural 19th- and 20th-century American scenes and still lifes. His favorite subject, though, is the eagle, which he's been painting and studying for years. "It still is a thrill to be at an eagle sighting and to hear his shrill cry. His come-back story is one we can be proud of," says the artist, who supports many conservation groups, including Wildlife for Tomorrow, Pheasants Forever, Rocky Mountain Elk Foundation, Quail Unlimited and Arizona Nestwatch.

Blaylock's work has been reproduced by The Franklin Mint, and published as prints and Giclées by Blaylock Originals, Inc. The artist, who lives with his family in Mesa, Arizona, has a distinctive signature: There's a cross above the letter "C" in front of his name. It is his testimony of God's love in his life, and has been included in his signature since 1971, when God answered his prayers and healed his wife, Norma, who was seriously ill.

"Ridge Patrol" is 30½ inches wide by 26 inches wide. It has been published by Blaylock Originals, Inc. in a limited edition of 300. "Anasaz Nestbuilder III," opposite page, is 24 inches wide by 33½ inches high, has been published in a limited edition of 950. The artist sells his originals for between $2,000 and $50,000.

Collin Bogle

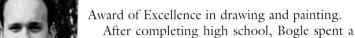

I'm crazy about fishing, and I get some of my best ideas for paintings when I am out on a lake in the early morning or late evening, when the lake is calm and quiet. Also, on the way to these lakes, I often spot good foliage for composing an idea," says Collin Bogle. Born in Seattle, in 1973, and still a resident of the Evergreen State, Bogle is surrounded by the majesty and beauty of nature. Washington boasts more than 1.9 million acres of state forest and 215 state parks—providing a great playground for young Bogle and his mountain bike, and an ideal source of inspiration for the wildlife paintings he does today.

Like the great outdoors, art was very much a part of Bogle's youth, as his father was a renowned artist and teacher. The youngster didn't think about following in his father's footsteps, though, until he was in high school. Then, in art classes taught by his father, Bogle's own talent blossomed. Techniques, such as painting perspective, that others struggled with seemed to come naturally to him. Classmates dubbed him "the artist," and his high school honored him at graduation with its Award of Excellence in drawing and painting.

After completing high school, Bogle spent a summer working as an apprentice for his father. His love of art and his obvious abilities made him realize that he, too, could pursue a career as a painter. He was doing a lot of portrait painting when he came upon the work of contemporary wildlife artists and found it fascinating. He thought wildlife might make a nice change from portraiture, and quickly found that he liked "painting the detail in nature and making the animals come to life with detail in the hair and eyes." Bogle hopes that viewers of his paintings will "see an animal in the wild in a way that they would not normally see it—up close, and with beautiful detail and lighting."

Bogle finds his subjects in wildlife parks and zoos, where he spends hours getting to know how they behave and taking hundreds of reference photos. "You can see a lot in your local zoo," he says, "if you go enough. One of my favorite sightings was watching a snow leopard stalk and chase a bird in a tree. I've also seen a mountain lion climb 40 feet up a tree in a couple of seconds."

Powerful animals, such as wolves, lions and bears, have special appeal to Bogle. "I like to paint wolves because of their behavior and likeness to dogs," he says. "I love to paint the mane of a lion," he adds, noting that he enjoys the challenge of painting hair.

The artist uses various mediums—including acrylics, pastels, colored pencils—to achieve his photo-realistic paintings, with emphasis on lighting and drama. His originals sell for between $500 and $10,000 each. Affordable prints of his work have been published by Hadley House of Bloomington, Minnesota, since 1996.

Collin Bogle's "Northern Exposure," 26¾ inches wide by 18 inches high, is limited to a signed and numbered edition of 999. The artist enjoys creating specific moods for his detailed portraits of wildlife, which he does with a strong, yet subtle, use of illumination. "Autumn Eyes," opposite page, is 14 inches wide by 20 inches high; its edition is limited to 1,500 signed and numbered prints.

His paintings also grace porcelain collector plates. Because of the popularity of his plate art, Bogle was honored with the 1998 Collectors' Choice New Artist of the Year award presented by The Bradford Exchange of Niles, Illinois.

Carl Brenders

Carl Brenders believes that everything in nature is perfect. "That is why I paint the way I do, with so much detail and so much realism," he says. "I want to capture that perfection." Combining an intimate knowledge of his subject with attention to even the smallest of details, Brenders provides us with an up-close and personal view of the world of nature as it is seldom seen. "A painter is a privileged being, because in his imagination he can come very close to the animals he paints. In reality, one can never come this close to wild animals, particularly if they are predators," Brenders explains.

Born near Antwerp, Belgium, in 1937, Brenders began drawing in childhood and has never stopped. He studied

Personnel from Mill Pond Press saw his work at that show and began issuing limited-edition prints of his paintings shortly thereafter. To date, the Venice, Florida, publisher has reproduced more than 100 of Brenders' paintings as prints on paper and canvas.

To create his mixed-media paintings—Brenders uses a combination of watercolor and gouache—he first selects a subject or subjects from the tens of thousands of photos he's taken in the field. Then he begins to sketch, drawing his subjects from a variety of angles. Only when he has captured the essence of the animals in his sketches does he move to his painting surface. There, he draws his scene in detail before applying paint. He first paints his background, which is as important to him as the wildlife and the mood he creates in each of his artworks. Then he adds his amazingly lifelike birds and animals.

Today, Brenders is a favorite with collectors not just in the United States and Belgium, but also in Canada, France Germany, Spain, Holland, Argentina and Japan. The artist has received many awards and honors over the past two decades. Beginning in 1985, his work has regularly been included in the Leigh Yawkey Woodson Art Museum's "Birds in Art" exhibition, as well as in many of the museum's "Wildlife in Art" shows. The Carnegie Museum of Natural History in Pittsburgh, Pennsylvania,

Carl Brenders' "Up Close—Barred Owl" is 17¼ inches wide by 10¼ inches high. "Miles to Go," opposite page, has been published by Mill Pond Press in a limited edition of 4,500 signed and numbered prints. The print is 20⅞ inches wide by 31¼ inches high.

staged a retrospective exhibition of 30 of his works, which then traveled to museums in Cleveland, Louisville and Shreveport. His work has been featured in many wildlife art shows and is the subject of a book titled *Wildlife: The Nature Paintings of Carl Brenders*. In 1998, Brenders was inducted into the *U.S. Art* Hall of Fame.

at the Fine Arts Academy in Antwerp and later at Berchem. In the 1960s and '70s, Brenders worked as a commercial artist. Among his projects was creating wildlife illustrations for a series of books titled *The Secret Life of Animals*. The artist came to the attention of American collectors in 1983, when he exhibited his paintings at the Trailside Galleries in Jackson, Wyoming.

Brenders has traveled through Europe, North America and Africa, studying animals and their habitat. A dedicated conservationist, he notes that "this planet could be a paradise." His art, which focuses on "the wild beauty of this planet" helps to call attention to the need to preserve the world's animals and their habitat.

Carl Brenders' "Nosing Around" has been published by Mill Pond Press in a limited edition of 1,500 signed and numbered prints. The print is 23¾ inches wide by 34 inches high. "Mixed Company," left, is 28 inches wide by 21⅜ inches high. Brenders completed this mixed-media work in 2000.

Carel Pieter Brest van Kempen

I've painted all my life, but not always well," says Carel Pieter Brest van Kempen. "I began painting full-time in 1989—that's when I first showed my work in public. If you look at the stuff I did as an eight-year-old, though, you'll see similarities in theme to what I do today. Even when I was in my late teens and early 20s—when I thought I was Salvador Dali and tried to paint like him—my work was nature oriented."

Born in 1958, in Murray, Utah, Brest van Kempen spent his youth exploring the back country, training falcons and studying herpetology. He later studied biology at the University of Utah and Oregon State; his art education, however, was limited to a high school drawing class focusing on perspective. The artist honed his skills through long hours at his easel, helped by tips from fellow artists. He has been honored with the 1992 Arts for the Parks Wildlife Award, and Best of Show awards at the Southeastern Wildlife Art Expo, and at the 1995 and 1998 Pacific Rim Wildlife Art Shows.

He is a member of the Society of Animal Artists, and has received its highest honor, The Award of Excellence, in 1994, 1996 and 1997. His work is in the permanent collections of The Springville Art Museum in Utah, The Leigh Yawkey Woodson Art Museum in

"Hippopotamus & Nile Soft-shell Turtles," an acrylic on illustration board, is 30 inches wide by 20 inches high.

"Red-eyed Leaf Frog" is seven inches wide by seven inches high. It is from a series of 12 frog paintings Brest van Kempen did, each representing one of the 12 major frog families. "The red-eyed leaf frog is found in Central America," the artist notes. His "Caribbean Flamingo," left, is 15 inches wide by 40 inches high.

Wausau, Wisconsin, The World Center for Birds of Prey in Boise, Idaho, and Vermont's Bennington Center for the Arts. He has created the illustrations for a number of books, and prints of his paintings are published by Mill Pond Press, Venice, Florida.

Brest van Kempen's work is very tight, very detailed, what he describes as "organized clutter, with a lot going on—really complicated compositions." He consciously selects subjects that most wildlife artists overlook, and then paints them "involved in living their lives, rather than just sitting there looking pretty. I try to say something about the individual species that I'm depicting—to figure out what it is that makes it unique, and then to characterize that in my painting. Usually, it's some aspect of the animal's behavior, but it could be something as simple as the form and color of the animal." While he paints a variety of subjects, Brest van Kempen does have "pet" groups—wildlife

he particularly enjoys painting. They are primates, hornbills, reptiles and amphibians, and birds of prey.

"When I decide to do a particular painting, I generally have to do a whole lot of research before I start. That's the fun part of the work," says Brest van Kempen, who spends about two months a year in the field. Sometimes, ideas for paintings come while he is in the field, but take years to germinate. Such was the case with "Convoy Through the Canopy," a triptych that he completed in 2000. "I had the idea for this piece while trekking across Central Africa in 1996," he says. "For about three years, I worked on sketches to try to get all of the stuff I wanted into the piece and make it work as a coherent composition, and I just couldn't do it. Then I thought of breaking it up into three pieces—making it a triptych." It depicts a Central African rain forest canopy. "The viewer is in the canopy,

looking down on a little African village. In the foreground is a big fig tree with de Brazza's monkeys moving across the canopy from right to left," he explains. Also seen are long-tailed hornbills and oil-palm squirrels, "which like to follow monkeys around because the monkeys scare up a lot of food items for them."

Just as Brest van Kempen paints animals overlooked by most artists, he also supports conservation efforts that seldom claim the limelight. Among his pet programs: sustainable tropical agricultural research. "A lot of the problems about tropical deforestation have to do with the fact that most of these places are using European agricultural practices that don't work very well—practices adopted when the areas were colonized by Europeans," he explains.

Carel Pieter Brest van Kempen calls "Convoy Through the Canopy," this recently completed triptych, "the most ambitious and, I think, one of the best things I've ever done." The center piece is 30 by 30 inches; the two side panels are 20 inches wide by 30 inches high.

Darrell Bush

When Darrell Bush began painting full-time in 1990, his focus was animal portraiture. However, about midway into the decade he began to paint what he calls "wilderness art." He explains, "I've shifted the focus from the animal to man's association with wildlife and its natural surroundings." In some of his acrylics, such as "Shallow Crossing," it is the animal that first captures one's attention, but in others, you have to search for the wildlife—just as you must search for it in nature.

A nature-lover since childhood, Bush says, "My time spent in the outdoors, whether camping, fishing or hunting, gave me the memories I cherish the most. This love for the outdoors and all things wild naturally influenced or spilled over into my interest in art." Born in Moline, Illinois, in 1960, he enjoyed drawing as a child and painting as a teenager. He earned a B.F.A. degree from Northern Illinois University, Dekalb, after which he worked as commercial illustrator for five years. During that time, in 1987, he won the Upland Game Stamp competition.

Once Bush quit doing commercial artwork, he was able to spend more time in the natural world that he so loves. "On a research trip in Canada, I had the opportunity to feed a pair of bald eagles some of the fish I had caught. Bald eagles love handouts," he says, "and if you are patient enough, you can catch them on film lifting a fish right off the surface of the water. It is an exhilarating sight! But sometimes," he warns, "photographing wild animals can get a bit precarious. On a trip to Wyoming's Yellowstone Park, I got a little too close to a pair of rutting bull elk, who were sparring off. I began photographing a herd of elk, when I noticed the large bull was being challenged by a bull coming from behind me. Fortunately, I was next to my opened car door and could jump in at a moment. The large bull expressed his displeasure with my presence by banging his antlers on the car next to mine. He got his point across, and I kept my distance."

Currently, Bush is focusing on "pristine northern lake settings. The crystal-clear water and elusive wildlife pose new challenges and new inspiration," he says. The preservation of the animals and environments he paints is important to Bush, who is an active member of the National Audubon Society and Ducks Unlimited. He is also active in various conservation projects, and created the artwork for the 1996 National Fish and Wildlife Print, as well as for several Ducks Unlimited prints.

Bush's paintings have been featured in national magazines, including *Wildlife Art, U.S. Art, Midwest Today, Minnesota Waterfowler* and *Collector Editions*, and have won several Best of Show awards. He has also had his share of honors, including being named the 1997 Artist of the Year at the National Wildlife Western and Americana Art show in Minneapolis, Minnesota, and having his work included in the 1996 "Wonders of Nature" exhibit in Hong Kong. Bush's original acrylics on hardboard sell for between $1,000 and $15,000. Prints of his paintings have been published by Hadley House since 1991 and are available in about 3,000 galleries in the United States and Canada.

"A Midnight Clear" is 16½ inches wide by 22 inches high. It has been published by Hadley House in an open edition. "Shallow Crossing," opposite page, is 17 inches wide by 27¾ inches high. Hadley House has published it in a signed and numbered edition of 999 prints and 99 artist proofs.

Lee Cable

A cowboy at heart, Lee Cable's idea of a good time is getting dressed in late-1800s clothing, grabbing his guns, leaping on his horse, and riding like mad while shooting at balloons. This may sound a bit odd to anyone not familiar with the equestrian sport of Cowboy Mounted Shooting—a sport that the artist and his wife, professional writer Pam Dean Cable, enjoy and at which he, if not she, excels. He has competed in two World Finals; she's got the riding down pat, but straight shooting from the saddle seems to be a bit of a problem.

Born in Greenville, Ohio, in 1943, Cable was raised on a farm and learned about both nature and art from his father, who recognized his son's early talent. His talent was honed by nine years of private tutelage with painter Martin Wogoman; his understanding of nature was enhanced by years of hunting with his dad. As a young man, Cable worked as an art director—first at Greenville's Neff Athletic Lettering Company, and then at LEAP Advertising Agency in Lakeland, Florida—and as an editorial artist for Florida's *Tampa Times* newspaper. Then in 1974, he quit his newspaper job to paint full-time. "This move was against the sage advice of many," he says, but he was determined to be a successful wildlife and Western art painter.

Cable's career since then has been impressive. He's been a featured artist at about a dozen of America's top shows. He's won the 1982-83 Florida Waterfowl Stamp competition and the 1988-89 South Carolina Waterfowl Stamp contest. His work has been featured in five of Leigh Yawkey Woodson's prestigious "Birds in Art" exhibitions and in many national magazines, including *Sporting Classics, U.S. Art, Wildlife Art News, Collector Editions, Art Impressions* and *The Conservationist*.

His artwork has appeared on collector plates from The Bradford Exchange and The Danbury Mint. It has graced steins from the National Wild Turkey Federation; greeting cards, tiles, magnets, T-shirts and gift bags from Leanin' Tree; porcelains from Lenox Collectibles; and home decor items from Toland Enterprises. The Franklin

"Buffalo Trace" is 48 inches wide by 24 inches high. This painting of bison is an original oil.

"Golden Slippers—Snowy Egrets" is 36 inches wide by 24 inches high. "The Silent Guardian—Snow Leopard," right, is 30 inches wide by 20 inches high.

Mint has issued limited-edition prints of his paintings, and a variety of companies have featured his wildlife art on note cards.

In talking about his style, Cable says, "I started out a little on the impressionistic side, went to photo-realism and now am going back to a more contemporary portrayal." Cable paints with various mediums—from gouache to oil; his originals sell for $1,200 to $20,000 each, but prints of his paintings are available. He hopes that viewers of his art gain "an appreciation for the natural beauty of animals and their adaptability in nature. They all have an intelligence that many can't seem to comprehend. Hopefully, my artwork will elicit some knowledge of that." On a personal level, he's admits to a fascination with wolves and coyotes "because of their beautiful coats, their intelligence and their family lifestyle. I'm also infatuated with the bison. They are a challenge to paint," he adds. The riding horses that the artist and his wife keep "have inspired me to paint them, too," says Cable, "along with the ranch scenes around our mountain home in Divide, Colorado."

Guy Coheleach

He's an artist and an adventurer, a conservationist and a philanthropist. His name is Guy Coheleach, and he is one of America's best-known and top-selling wildlife artists.

Born in New York City in 1933, Coheleach is a graduate of New York City's Cooper Union and holds an honorary doctorate from William & Mary College. He is perhaps best known for his paintings of big cats, in part because of the popularity of *The Big Cats: The Paintings of Guy Coheleach*, one of three books featuring his artwork, and a Book-of-the-Month Club selection in 1982. The other books are *Coheleach: Master of the Wild* and *Guy Coheleach's Animal Art*. The artist, however, paints a wide variety of animals and birds. Our government has given his "American Eagle" print to visiting heads of state, and the Leigh Yawkey Woodson Art Museum recognized the excellence of his artworks depicting birds when it honored Coheleach as Master Artist at its 1983 "Birds in Art" exhibition.

A member of the Adventurer's Club of New York and a fellow of the Explorer's Club, Coheleach gets to pursue his love of adventure through his professional need to spend time in the world's wilderness areas studying the subjects of his art. He has traveled extensively through the United States, Europe, South America and Africa—sometimes visiting Africa as many as four times in one year. The animals and settings in his artworks are so vibrant, so lifelike, because he knows them so well. His close encounters with wild animals are, he says, "too many" to mention, but they include being run down by an elephant in Zambia—a 1972 experience that was captured on film and shown on national television.

The celebrated artist is the subject of two films: *Guy Coheleach and the Bald Eagle* and *Quest: An Artist and His Prey*. He and his work have also been featured in numerous national magazines, including *Reader's Digest, Saturday Evening Post, Audubon, National Wildlife* and *Wildlife Art News*. He is a member of the Society of Animal Artists, and has received its Award of Excellence eight times. The artist is especially proud of this award, as its recipient is selected by museum curators and university professors of fine art.

Coheleach has had his work featured in one-man shows at a number of major American museums, including The Carnegie Museum in Pittsburgh and The Newark Museum, as well as at art galleries across the country. His work has also been exhibited at the National Collection of Fine Art, The White House, The Corcoran Gallery, and Canada's Royal Ontario Museum. Prints of his artworks are published by Mill Pond Press, Venice, Florida.

Coheleach helps supports many conservation groups. Also, he has given an endowment to the University of Tennessee; it is used to provide scholarships for students of wildlife management.

Guy Coheleach's "Siberian Summer" is an original acrylic on Masonite. It is 40 inches wide by 30 inches high.

An oil on canvas, Guy Coheleach's "Eye to Eye" is 36 inches wide by 60 inches high.

Simon Combes

Born in Shaftesbury, England, in 1940, Simon Combes moved to Kenya at age six. Sailing from England to Mombassa was a "real adventure" for Combes, who spent much of it "balancing on the top rail of the deck. Before leaving England, I had always been in trouble, wandering off and getting lost in the woods. This was better than the woods, but the two-day journey by train from Mombassa to Nakuru, where we had a farm, was the one that impacted my life. It was a journey through a great wilderness filled with every conceivable wild animal, all easily visible from the carriage window. I became instantly hooked on Africa and its wildlife."

Combes became a citizen of Kenya and lives there about six months of each year. "I rent a house on a 58,000-acre ranch owned by Lord Delamere in the Great Rift Valley. My father worked for his father when I was a teenager, so this is like home." In Kenya, he divides his time between painting and researching the animals he loves, taking photos and sketching. "The Nakuru National Park, where I can sit with rhinos, lions, leopards and many other species of wildlife, is just ten minutes from my house. Often, I will visit this place just for a few hours in the early morning. I have many favorite places, but this is near the top of the list." When not in Kenya, Combes may be found in the United States, painting in his Idaho apartment, or traveling the world in search of animals to paint.

A self-taught artist, Combes began painting as a hobby while in the Kenya military. "When Kenya was a British colony, until December 1963, the colonial governor maintained a small local force known as the Kenya Regiment. All white males were required to do six months of military training as soon as they reached the age of 18," Combes explains. After his six months of mandatory service, he applied for and got an officer's commission in the Kings African Rifles—a regiment that existed in all the British colonies in eastern Africa. His goal was not an army career, however, but rather to see the world "at someone else's expense." For his training, Combes was sent to Uganda, where one of his duties was to "knock the rough edges off Idi Amin and teach him some of the qualities of an officer and gentleman. I didn't do a very good job." Later, he was sent to England's Royal Military Academy Sandhurst, from which he graduated in 1962.

While stationed in northern Kenya, "where I was involved in a guerrilla war against Somali secessionists," Combes relaxed by drawing the nomadic people of the area. Eventually, he began painting in oils, which remain his medium of choice, and depicting the animals that he so loves. His fastidious insistence on accuracy, combined with an intimate knowledge of his subjects,

"Heavy Drinkers," 58½ inches wide by 25 inches high, has been published by The Greenwich Workshop in a signed and numbered edition of 550. Combes hopes his paintings "make people stop in their tracks, do a double-take and say, 'Wow!' I would like them to see how perfect nature is; to ask questions about what is going on in this painting; to arouse curiosity and awareness; to realize how precious these dwindling natural treasures are."

"There Was a Time," above, is 74 inches wide by 27¼ inches high. It has been issued as a Greenwich Workshop Masterwork Fine Art Canvas, enhanced with the artist's original brushstrokes, and is limited to an edition of 250 signed and numbered pieces. "Eyes of Warning," top, is 29 inches wide by 21¼ inches high. It has been published by The Greenwich Workshop in a signed and numbered edition of 950. "I have a special affinity with cats. All kinds of cats," says Simon Combes. "I admire many of their qualities—their beauty, stealth, independence, ability to relax....It may seem far-fetched, but I seem to affect cats in some way. They either love me or hate me. In a zoo in England, where I was doing some research, an Indian tiger dogged me all day, tried to get as close as it could, never let its eyes off me. The keeper, who had known this animal for years, wanted to know what I had done. I had done nothing. There was some kind of chemistry going on. In a similar place in the United States, when I stood in front of a snow leopard's cage, it flew at the bars, snarling and spitting. The owner was astonished. She had raised this animal from a kitten and never seen it show any aggression. Why me? Again, I had done absolutely nothing."

make his paintings and prints—issued by The Greenwich Workshop, Shelton, Connecticut—true celebrations of nature.

Becoming a self-supporting, full-time artist, after spending 15 years as a professional soldier/paratrooper, could not have been easy, but that's not his only accomplishment. Combes is also an author. "I have always wanted to write," he says. "The release of my first book, *An African Experience*, is something of which I am unashamedly proud."

Chris Cummings

I got interested in depicting wildlife originally because I was working as a wildlife biologist and enjoyed sketching and painting the animals I routinely saw, such as deer, pronghorn, squirrels, birds and hawks," says Chris Cummings. Later, after she and her husband, Larry, bought a farm in Oregon's Willamette Valley, she began painting horses, and they are now her primary subject and one she knows very well. "I ride my horses a lot, and take them camping and packing into the mountains," she says. "I also belong to a statewide riding club that builds and maintains campgrounds and trails for horses, and lobbies the government on behalf of horse owners." The artist and mother of three is also an active member of The Nature Conservancy.

Originally from California—she was born in Los Angeles in 1948—Cummings spent two years as an art major at the University of California, Santa Barbara, before transferring to Humbolt State University, located in Arcata, California. The change in schools also marked her change in majors: she earned a degree in wildlife biology, but had a minor in fine art. "I started drawing as soon as I could hold a pencil, and was a temperamental artist by the time I hit kindergarten. I can't remember what my motivation was then, other than I really enjoyed drawing, which still

holds true today," she says.

Cummings uses oils to create her paintings, which she describes as "realistic, without being photographic. I like a sense of drama and mood, created either through the use of lighting or action. The horses are always the focal point and must be expressive. I pay a lot of attention to that," she explains. The artist owns or has owned most of the horses seen in her painting; these include thoroughbreds, quarter horses, appaloosas, ponies, a pinto and her new Tennessee Walker. "If I need a particular type of horse that I don't have, then I will try and locate one that the owner will allow me to work with," she says. "All of my draft horse references come from years of attending plowing matches and draft horse shows, plus commission work I've done for draft horse breeders."

While you might think that horses make a pretty safe subject when compared to the wild animals of Africa, that's not necessarily the case. "I have been trampled by running horses three times, have been knocked off by tree limbs and storm drains, and have just plain fallen off more times than I care to count. I also had my two front teeth kicked out," says the artist.

Cummings has had her work featured in *Equine Images, Farm Woman News, Morgan Horse Today, Tennessee Walker* and *The Reach* magazines. She has illustrated children's books and created artwork for greeting cards and calendars. Limited-edition prints of her paintings are published by Wild Wings, Lake City, Minnesota. Her originals, which sell for $3,000 to $18,000 each, are found in private and public collections across the country, including the collections of Oregon State University and the University of California, in Santa Barbara. Her prints are available at galleries nationwide.

"Approaching Storm Triptych" has been published by Wild Wings in an edition of 1,200. The central piece, left, is 27 inches wide by 18 inches high; the two outer paintings are 13½ inches wide by 18 inches high.

Robert Deurloo

On Highway 93, just outside Salmon, Idaho, stands a large bronze sculpture of a bear swiping at three salmon that appear to be leaping upstream. This dramatic creation is by renowned wildlife artist Robert Deurloo, who has been a resident of Salmon, population 2,941, since the early 1990s. Just ten miles from the Continental Divide and adjacent to the largest wilderness area in the lower 48 states, the tiny town of Salmon is the perfect place for the artist, since most of his subjects, says Deurloo, "live within ten minutes of my home."

A Westerner by birth as well as by choice—Deurloo was born in San Francisco, California, in 1946, and raised in Colorado—he developed a love of wildlife from years of living amongst it. He continues to spend hours "in the field" observing the birds and beasts he depicts in his artworks: bison, bears, ducks, deer, antelope, otters, foxes, cougars, elk. Of these, Deurloo's favorite to feature are elk. "I think they are one of the most majestic animals in North America, and I observe them in the wild almost daily," he says. This isn't surprising since Idaho, as game hunters know, boasts the largest elk herds in the United States.

Deurloo, who holds degrees from the Colorado School of Mines and Harvard's Graduate School of Business, is a self-taught artist. He realized his sculpting talent after seeing a bronze sculpture that he wanted, but couldn't afford, so decided to make his own. He cast his first antelope in 1977. Since then, Deurloo has perfected his sculpting style and mastered the process of casting his creations from molten bronze. He also has learned that highly realistic works, which he initially created, are not necessarily the best. Today, rather than trying to depict every hair and feather of his subjects, he concentrates on capturing their essence and spirit. "This is more difficult and spiritual than a mechanical reproduction," says the artist and ardent conservationist, who hopes that his work will inspire others to form spiritual connections with our natural environment and fellow creatures. Among the conservation groups that the artist helps support are the Rocky Mountain Elk Foundation and Ducks Unlimited.

In addition to the almost impressionistic style of Deurloo's bronzes, they are distinguished by the artist's unique use of patinas. Created by a combination of intense heat, various acids and minerals, the patinas give his bronzes the appearance of polished stone—and not just any stone; they look as if they were chiseled out of the granite that is found in the Sawtooth Mountains of central Idaho.

Deurloo's limited-edition bronzes sell for between $300 and $5,000 each, and can be found in some 60 galleries here and abroad. The artist also exhibits at about 20 wildlife shows a year, at which he's received many awards. Deurloo was honored as the Featured Sculptor at the 1998 National Zoological Society in Washington, D.C., and his 14-inch-high bronze bison titled "Prairie Patriarch" is on permanent display at the Smithsonian Institution's National Museum of American Art, Washington, D.C.

"Sawtooth Sentinels" is 13 inches high and limited to an edition of 100; it depicts members of a wolf pack near the rugged Sawtooth Mountains of central Idaho.

"Intruder!" is 20 inches high and limited to an edition of 100. Through the use of patinas, the artist has made this bronze sculpture of elk appear as if it were chiseled from a piece of stone. "Bison," right, is seven inches high and limited to an edition of 1,000 pieces. Created as a tribute to the former rulers of the prairie, this Deurloo bronze captures the bison's majesty and mystery.

Les Didier

An aunt inspired Les Didier's early interest in art. "She was a very gifted artist, and took me with her to art classes," he explains. Because of her influence, Didier decided he wanted to be a commercial illustrator. He took art classes in high school, and upon graduation, attended the art institute in his hometown of Dayton, Ohio. However, he left the Dayton Art Institute before graduating in order to accept a job in the graphic arts field. His career was interrupted by four years in the United States Air Force, although, there, too, his graphic arts skills were utilized. In 1957, upon leaving the service, Didier moved to Milwaukee and got work as an advertising art illustrator. He formed his own advertising art studio in 1964.

Didier's business was successful, but not as personally fulfilling as the artist had anticipated. He soon realized that he "needed a diversion from commercial illustration and running my own commercial studio. I attended some shows by Owen Gromme, and also met him on several occasions. He inspired me, because he was doing some of his best work in his 60s and beyond, and I wasn't getting any younger." Finding ample subjects in Wisconsin's more than 14,000 lakes, its forests and its woods, Didier began painting birds. His favorite are raptors, which he gets many commissions to paint, but he also excels at capturing the unique natures and beauty of songbirds and waterfowl. "I try to depict the birds fairly realistically," Didier says, "and generally use an impressionistic background." He sees his completed works as blendings of the imagery of mind and senses. His medium of choice is acrylic.

Didier sold his graphic arts business in 1990, in order to devote more time to painting, which is what he most enjoys doing. He also gets pleasure from observing his subjects and photographing them for later reference. Didier does additional research in his local library, and, he says, "I have a pretty good reference library of my own." He won the 1995 and 1998 Wisconsin Duck Stamp competitions, and his paintings have been included in four of the prestigious "Birds in Art" exhibitions at the Leigh Yawkey Woodson Museum, located in Wausau, Wisconsin. In 1986, he was honored as Artist of the Year for Milwaukee's PBS Channel 10. Like many of his fellow wildlife painters, Didier is an avid conservationist. Among the groups he helps support are the Wisconsin Waterfowlers, Ducks Unlimited and Friends of the Field.

The artist's original paintings are in numerous private and corporate collections. Limited-edition prints of Didier's paintings have been available since 1985. They are published by Hadley House, Bloomington, Minnesota, and are found in galleries across the country. His paintings have also been featured on collector plates. Didier's first plate, "Quite Water," was issued in 1987; his "Winter Grotto" plate was issued the following year. The artist personally exhibits at several wildlife shows each year, and his work is regularly featured at the Biannual Wildlife Art Show at the Miller Art Museum, located in Sturgeon Bay, Wisconsin.

"On Silent Wings" is 18 inches wide by 24 inches high. Hadley House has published it in a signed and numbered edition of 999. A single hummingbird is the focus of Les Didier's "Summer Jewel," opposite page. This 9-inch-wide by 12-inch-high print has been published in a limited, signed and numbered edition of 850. As these artworks show, Didier's birds are very realistic, but his backgrounds tend to be more impressionistic.

Adele Earnshaw

Working in transparent watercolors, Adele Earnshaw concentrates on design and composition. "I often use manmade elements for the strong shapes that are important in my designs," she says, noting that in many of her paintings the birds are not immediately noticed. "I use the design of the painting to bring the viewer's eye to the bird, so that when it is seen, it's often a nice surprise." Although the manmade items in Earnshaw's paintings are the result of her search for strong composition, they remind us that wildlife is found not only in fields and forests—that it also exists in urban areas, in our backyards and on our city streets.

Earnshaw's interest in wildlife stems from her childhood in New Zealand; she was born in Hastings, in 1949, and lived in Warkworth until age 12, when her family emigrated to the United States. "New Zealand is a country of birds," she says. "Because I grew up in a rural area, on an estuary surrounded by native bush, and because New Zealand schools teach nature studies, I was always interested in the natural world."

Surprisingly, while she always enjoyed doing handicrafts, she had no idea she could paint until she took a beginning watercolor class at age 25. She then set a goal for herself: "I wanted my work to be recognizable as mine, without my signature." She says her art has been influenced "by the work of Frances Lee Jacques and N.C. Wyeth, and by my peers and friends, Lindsay Scott and Joe Garcia."

A member of the Society of Animal Artists, Earnshaw exhibits her work at wildlife art shows around the country. Her paintings have also been featured at New York City's Museum of Natural History, and at the National Museum of History in Taipei, and they've been included in eight of the Leigh Yawkey Woodson Museum's "Birds in Art" exhibits. The honor that she is perhaps proudest of, however, is having her paintings selected for New Zealand's first three Game Bird Habitat Stamps. "The funds generated by this stamp program go towards conservation, which will help me repay my debt to New Zealand. It is because of my childhood in New Zealand that I love birds and nature. I am honored to have a part in saving it," she says. Earnshaw supports conservation efforts in more than her native country, donating prints to a variety of groups, including chapters of the Audubon Society and Ducks Unlimited.

Earnshaw currently resides in Sedona, Arizona, and is an avid gardener. Flowers from her garden appear in some of her artworks, as do the birds in her backyard. "I have five species of hummingbirds at my feeder," she says. Her research also takes her to museums, zoos and nature parks. "The Arizona Sonora Desert Museum in Tucson has a great aviary and hummingbird house," she says. Other places she especially enjoys: the Minneapolis and San Diego zoos; the Wild Animal Park in Escondido, California; the Blackwater Refuge in Cambridge, Maryland; New Zealand's many parks and refuges; and the Fu-Shan Nature Reserve in Taiwan.

The artist and her work have been featured in a number of magazines, including *American Artist Publication*, *U.S. Art*, *Wildlife Art Magazine* and *Collector Editions*. Prints of her original watercolors are published by Hadley House, Bloomington, Minnesota.

"Santuario de Guadalupe" is 19 inches wide by 48 inches high. Earnshaw feels that setting her birds among the stronger, larger shapes of manmade objects strengthens her compositions. She also likes "the element of surprise viewers often get when the bird is seen, when the painting is understood." (Photo of artist: Canby Photography)

"Tree Sparrows at Dragon Mountain," 27½ inches wide by 13 inches high, was inspired by the Dragon Mountain Temple in downtown Taipei. The artist visited Taiwan in 1999, at the time her work and that of 12 other artists from around the world was exhibited at the National Museum of History in Taipei. "The Roost," top, is 34 inches wide by 34 inches high.

Jim Eppler

Painter and sculptor Jim Eppler readily admits to having a romance with "the play of light and shadow, the way paint builds on canvas." He is equally captivated by gestures and textures that lend themselves to the three-dimensional aspect of bronzes. "My art," he says, "is simply an expression of my passion for painting and sculpting, with wildlife being a favorite subject. A finished piece of my art is a gift which has been given to me, and is offered to others who share my love of wildlife." The emotion that he hopes viewers of his work will experience is "pure enjoyment. If my art can hold someone's attention and capture their imagination, I am pleased," he says.

Born in Oakland, California, in 1950, Eppler became fascinated with the animal world as a child. He kept a menagerie of pets and spent endless hours hiking through the desert looking for creatures, which he'd then draw or paint. His interest in wildlife has matured since then, leading him to an understanding of animals' complex role in our world and an appreciation for their many contributions to life on this planet. In his paintings and bronzes, Eppler depicts a variety of wildlife, because, he says, "Each animal is inspiring in its own

"'Symbol' Bison" is 11¾ inches high, 18¾ inches long and 8 inches deep. The bronze sculpture is limited to an edition of 35.

SYMBOL
BISON
JIM EPPLER

"'Morning Light' Moose" is 40 inches wide and 30 inches high. Eppler has reproduced this original oil in a limited edition of 75 Giclées on canvas. "'Apparition' Whitetail," right, is an eleven-inch-high bronze sculpture, limited to an edition of 35.

right. I find myself being captivated by the characteristics of each species that I study to paint or sculpt."

The artist's childhood joy in hiking and hunting for animal life has continued into adulthood, too. Now, though, he travels further afield and totes camping gear and photography equipment along with his sketch pad. On his treks to deserts, mountains and plains, Eppler watches, listens, learns and captures on film the remarkable dimensions of wildlife and their habitats. "My photos reveal their form and habits, but their gift to my soul is what inspires me to paint and sculpt," he says.

Eppler earned a B.F.A. degree in Studio Art from Texas Tech University, located in Lubbock, Texas, which is where the artist now lives. He has also studied with Bob Kuhn, Robert Wood, Bill Worrell, Raymond Froman, Charles Reid and Paul Milosevich. Eppler's original oils, which he describes as "painterly," bring up to $8,500; Giclée-on-canvas reproductions of them are available for under $1,000 each. The artist's bronzes sell for between $350 and $3,300 each. The artist personally hand-finishes each of his bronze sculptures, using patinas and paint to denote the species distinctive markings. While he receives many invitations to wildlife shows, he devotes most of his time to commissioned work and work for his galleries, located throughout the Southwest. Examples of his work are also found in the West Texas Ranching Heritage Museum, the West Texas Museum Collection, the Nashville Songwriters Hall of Fame, and in many corporate and private collections.

Like so many of his fellow wildlife artists, Eppler supports conservation efforts and strives to bring public attention to the importance of our animal life. Two organizations that are especially close to his heart are the National Museum of Wildlife Art and South Plains Wildlife Rehabilitation.

Lindsey Foggett

orn in Britain in 1962 and raised in the rural countryside of central England, Lindsey Foggett was fascinated by animals and the natural environment around her "as far back as I can remember. By the time I was seven or eight years old, I was pretty adamant that I was going to be a wildlife artist." Because, Foggett explains, "a passion to paint has been in my family for a number of generations," her interest in art was encouraged by her parents, who began taking her on painting and sketching outings when she was a very small child.

At age 19, the self-taught artist left home with 50 pounds in her pocket, determined to spend her life painting wildlife. And that's exactly what she's been doing ever since. She admits that her life as an artist hasn't always been easy, but quickly adds that "it has been tremendously fun and rewarding."

Foggett currently resides in the San Bernardino Mountains of Southern California. "My home is in a national park, and consequently I have wonderful inspiration on my doorstep, including bears, raccoons, bobcats, cougar, deer. But I also travel extensively to national parks all across the country, hiking, backpacking, sketching and taking all of my own reference pho-

tographs." To give you an idea of the number of reference photos Foggett has, in just one year (1999), she took 3,500 photographs in Yellowstone and another 3,000 in Alaska. She also visits game parks and rehabilitation centers, where she is able to get close to large predators. Occasionally, she will even go into cages with wolves, cougars, bobcats and other wild animals in order to get close-up shots.

Foggett's interest in wildlife has taken her on field trips throughout Europe and into Eastern Africa, too, but her primary interest is North American wildlife, especially the predators. "I focus on the large predators, many of which are threatened, and portray their gentler nature, their softer side, in the hopes that my art will inspire others to want to protect and save these magnificent creatures. They are highly complex animals with a strong, nurturing side, not just hunting machines," the artist notes.

While she has no favorite animal, the artist says there is nothing like the snow leopard "for sheer embodiment of power and beauty." The animal that constantly

"In Search of Spring," an original acrylic of a black bear, is 36 inches wide and 17½ inches high.

Lindsey Foggett's "Harmony" is 28 inches wide by 16⅛ inches high and limited to a signed and numbered edition of 999 prints. The Giclée of Foggett's "Green Reflections," right, is limited to an edition of 250. Featuring a bobcat, it is 9 inches wide by 12 inches high. "I enjoy painting a wide variety of animals, but I must confess to a preoccupation with the predators," says the artist. "I find them quite intriguing, partly because they are so elusive to study. I can still vivdly recall the thrill of spotting my first wolf in the wild, not more than 30 feet away!"

inspires here, though, is the wolf, which she finds "totally captivating." The hot subject for wildlife art in the 1990s, wolves have been "painted to exhaustion," says Foggett, thus as subjects they present a "constant challenge to create something new. But the complexity and intellectual nature of this animal always draws me into the next painting."

Preferring to use acrylics, Foggett portrays wildlife in soft, muted colors, "often on the cool side," she notes. She paints in a realistic style, paying great attention to detail on the animals. Her originals sell for between $900 and $16,000. Prints of her artworks are published by Hadley House, Bloomington, Minnesota. Foggett exhibits at a number of wildlife art shows each year, and was honored as a featured artist at the March 2000 Florida Wildlife Exposition. Her work can be found in galleries throughout the United States, as well as in Europe and Hong Kong.

Eric Forlee

I like to get as close to dangerous game as possible to get excited, to get the adrenaline pumping. I especially enjoy doing this with elephants that are near rivers. When an elephant charges, it usually stops at the banks of a river to avoid a fall and injury. The excitement guarantees that I'll have a great inspiration to create a new painting," says Eric Forlee. Sometimes, though, the artist is just minding his own business when excitement comes his way. "One cool September day, I was studying elephants at the Manapools National Park in northwestern Zimbabwe. An old, gentle elephant bull walked very slowly toward me; he was so close I could see the hair on his trunk. It was lovely. The situation was totally out of mind until the bull started to charge. I have never run so fast in my life.

and Communist indoctrination, Forlee escaped and made his way to Hong Kong. He did manual work, studied English and dreamed of Africa. After a time, his wife, whom he'd met and married in the camp, joined him in Hong Kong.

During his youth, Forlee had consumed books about Africa. When he was 30, he went to South Africa, to manage his father's business. He began painting the country's landscapes, and longed to stay, but was forced to return to Hong Kong after six months because of South Africa's immigration laws. He got a commercial art job in Hong Kong, but eventually he and his family moved to Zimbabwe. The landscapes he did there quickly sold, and soon he was able to support himself with his art. When he began painting wildlife, he gained international recognition. He was honored by the Michigan Wildlife Fund Foundation as its 1994 Artist of the Year, and by the Safari Club International Sacramento as Artist of the Year in 1994, 1995 and 1997. He was the Safari Club International's Artist of the Year in 1996.

Forlee is now a United States citizen, but regularly visits Zimbabwe, where he sees wild animals daily. "But without so many friends, national park wardens and professional animal management personnel, I would not be able to get close to the animals and into their natural environment to study them. I would never be able to paint them right. My paintings are full of life, because I study the subjects from life, not from photos," says Forlee. "When I paint, I am not just putting color on canvas. I am putting life and personal experience on a screen that will last many, many years after I have gone," he adds.

I jumped into the nearby river for safety—leaving the bull with my shirt in his trunk!"

Born in Moiyan, China, in 1949, Forlee loved to draw, and could do so "with great ease. Perhaps growing up as an orphan and having a bitter childhood drove me, with much imagination of the bright side of life that I missed so much," says the self-taught artist. His father lived in Africa, and when Forlee was seven, his mother move there, too, leaving Forlee to be raised in China by grandparents. At the age of 19, he was put into one of Mao Tse-Tung's re-education camps, because his ancestors had been landowners. After six years of hard labor

"Domination," an original oil on canvas, is 48 inches wide by 26 inches high. Eric Forlee's original oils sell for between $1,500 and $60,000. Prints of his paintings are published by Blackhawk Editions, Danville, California. Opposite page: "Lion Cubs" is 14 inches wide by 8 inches high; "Water Hole" is 48 inches wide by 26 inches high. "I have a great love for elephants," says Forlee. "They have so many characteristics, almost like human beings. They are powerful. They are strong, but they do not threaten anybody unless they are being threatened. They are gentle giants!"

Rod Frederick

"This would be an ideal job if it weren't for all the painting," jokes Rod Frederick, who admits to a wanderlust and an intrigue with world wildlife and the interaction of animals and their landscape. Fortunately, he always feels the pull to preserve the wildlife he observes, with his paintings and his support of conservation groups, such as Water for Wildlife, Rocky Mountain Elk and Ducks Unlimited.

Born in Salem, Oregon, in 1956, and a resident of that state except for a few of his very early years—when his father went to law school in Wisconsin—Frederick notes that "wildlife was something that was always right there." He began drawing it as a youth, and went on to earn a degree in art, with a minor in biology, from Salem's Willamette University. "I always combined my interest in animals and art," says Frederick.

Frederick has been painting professionally since college graduation. Initially, he did a lot of Pacific Northwest scenes, but he soon found himself focusing on wildlife. "Every landscape I paint has some kind of wildlife in it," he says, "even though the birds and animals may not be dominating the scene." He calls his style "romantic realism," noting that he has "a lot of light play and landscape" in his paintings. He finds inspiration by immersing himself in the outdoors, "in the places where animals are likely to be found. I think it's really important for an artist to paint what he knows, and my attempt is certainly to do that. So I spend a lot of time hiking—not just riding around in cars, although you can get a lot of ideas like that, too—hiking and getting the feel of bad weather and good weather and the combination. I think that in order to be a good artist,

Rod Frederick's "The High and the Mighty" has been published by Mill Pond Press as a Giclée on canvas; it is limited to 250 signed and numbered prints and 20 artist proofs. The print is 20 inches wide by 14 inches high. "Zebra Mirage," opposite page, is a Giclée printed on imported cotton rag paper. It is 30 inches wide by 17¼ inches high, and is limited to an edition of 250 signed and numbered pieces, plus 20 artist proofs.

you have to experience a lot," he adds.

In the field, Frederick takes numerous photographs and notes, plus does thumbnail sketches. Relying on these and his memory, he draws the background for his painting on stiff Belgium linen—which serves as his canvas. Once he's decided where to position the animals, he begins painting, using primarily oils and gouache. Frederick's paintings, published as limited-edition prints by Mill Pond Press, are complex works, usually containing multiple animals, often several species, with one dominating the scene.

"I paint a lot of North American birds and animals, but I've done a lot of African animals, too," says Frederick. "I'm currently working on a painting with some cockatoos in it, which are from Indonesia, so it's a little different. I've spent a lot of time in the Guatemala-Yucatan area exploring Mayan ruins and looking at tropical rain forests and tropical scrub land. In recent years,

I've done a number of paintings of the Mayan ruins, with the animals interacting with them."

While Frederick loves Africa and South America, he's also fond of the area around his Oregon home, located near Bend. "I like central Oregon a lot. I like the mountains. We're on the east side of the Cascade Range, so we get a lot of the storms coming off the Pacific. They hit the crest of mountains, deposit all their snow there, and what we get are these great sunsets. We get very little moisture, but we get really dramatic skies, and I paint them a lot," he says. He also paints a lot of elk. "It's not an intentional favorite, although I love watching elk—but I love all of the animals I see in the wild. I try to paint only animals I've seen in the wild, but I tend to gravitate toward elk. I've also painted wolves, antelope, mule deer, bald eagles—animals that we see in this area. But I don't restrict myself, because I always want an excuse to travel."

Joe Garcia

Joe Garcia specializes in painting birds, deer and other gentle creatures that reside in the forest of oaks and pines near his California home. A native Californian—he was born in Escondido in 1944—Garcia has created the artwork for three of his home state's conservation stamps: The 1993 California First of State Upland Game Bird Stamp, and the 1996-97 and 1999-2000 State of California Upland Game Bird Stamps. His artwork also graces the 1987 Quail Unlimited stamp, and he has been honored as Artist of the Year by a number of conservation organizations. Since 1993, his work has been featured in five of the Leigh Yawkey Woodson Art Museum's annual "Birds in Art" exhibitions. "Having work accepted into this internationally acclaimed show was a major accomplishment for me," he says.

The artist's love of wildlife springs from his childhood spent on a small ranch. "While growing up, I enjoyed the outdoors and always had an interaction with wildlife. Camping, hunting, surfing kept me involved with the natural surroundings." His interest in art began when he took general art classes in high school. "I discovered that I was able to create works of art that were enjoyed and appreciated by my family and friends. This gave me the impetus to think of art as a career," says Garcia. He attended Palomar Community College, then studied commercial art at the Art Center College of Design, Los Angeles, where he earned a B.F.A. degree. Next came 13 years of working as an illustrator and graphic designer.

During those years, he spent his free time painting. Then, in 1983, he began painting full-time, and it's a labor of love.

"I like to paint every day, when possible. When I see new subjects, I want to start a painting while the idea is fresh in my mind. I like doing small paintings, as well as large ones. Often smaller pieces are more exciting, because the medium can be controlled easier, allowing me to paint more spontaneously." Over the years, he says, his style of painting has evolved. "I originally painted the main subject with a lot of detail, and the background with a loose, interpretive style. I now do some paintings with the technique directed toward realism. I try to do the painting so that the technique captures the mood of the subject. I feel this interpretation of my reference is where I have grown." Garcia generally uses watercolors for his wildlife paintings. He also does plein air landscape paintings, and for them he uses oils.

"Family and friends have been the biggest influence in my art. I have always had great support," Garcia says. "When I started painting wildlife, friends and clients took me to areas where only a few people saw wildlife. They got me excited about what I was going to paint. They set the tone and direction of what I would do and paint in the future."

"Cotton Tail" is 18½ inches wide by 5½ inches high. Although Garcia generally uses watercolors for his wildlife paintings, this is an original oil on linen.

"Evening's Calm," left, is 10½ inches wide by 29 inches high; it has been published in a limited edition of 350 prints and 35 artist proofs. An original watercolor, "Odd Man Out" is 10½ inches wide by 28 inches high. "I like a viewer to look at my paintings and say, 'I've been there,' or 'I've seen that.' I like the subject to be correct in its setting or detail. I want the art to be pleasing to the eye and mind," says Joe Garcia.

Nancy Glazier

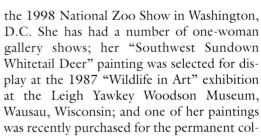

When Nancy Glazier was eight years old, her grandmother gave her a set of oil paints—"every color and tool a beginning painter could possibly need," says the artist. That gift marked the beginning of Glazier's "self-training and life's work." She sold her first painting at age 12. At age 16, she began studying with Cody Museum muralist Adolph Spohr. Later, to better understand the physical makeup of the animals that populate her paintings, Glazier took equine anatomy classes at Zahourek Systems. The classes, she says, involved a "hands-on 'kinesthetic' study from the bones up through every muscle, the deepest structures up to visible surface anatomy. It takes a tremendous amount of energy—very intensive."

Glazier says that she always knew she was an artist, and she always loved animals. "As a child, my pets were my soulmates," she recalls. "I had many small pets, and longed for horses and great dogs." When her family moved from Salt Lake City, Utah, to Cody, Wyoming, the teenager was able to visit the surrounding national parks and wildlife preserves. There she observed nature, photographed and sketched her subjects in their natural environments. As an adult, Glazier feels strongly about importance of first-hand experience with her subject matter. To become more at one with the animals she paints, she has milked goats, ridden horses, trained dogs and even raised buffalo. However, she prefers animals "to be truly wild and free." Experience, she says, "has taught me that if I am sensitive and respectful of the wild animals I observe, they accept my presence and exhibit all their natural behaviors. Once I experience the inseparable relationship between animal, environment, times and seasons, I am challenged to capture it on canvas."

Wildlife art at its best has an immediacy to it, a sense that if you blink, the animals will have moved or perhaps even disappeared from the setting. Glazier attains this immediacy by concentrating on the animals faces, noting that her emphasis is on "portraying the mood and the moment in that particular animal's life. I strive to capture that animal on that day in a certain light and in a certain circumstance." Then, rather than put the same detail in the area surrounding the animal, she says, "I complete the painting with a lot of abstract brush and palette knife work."

Glazier has received many honors for her paintings, including being the Featured Artist at the 1991 Pacific Rim Wildlife Art Show in Tacoma, Washington, and at the 1998 National Zoo Show in Washington, D.C. She has had a number of one-woman gallery shows; her "Southwest Sundown Whitetail Deer" painting was selected for display at the 1987 "Wildlife in Art" exhibition at the Leigh Yawkey Woodson Museum, Wausau, Wisconsin; and one of her paintings was recently purchased for the permanent collection of the National Museum of Wildlife Art, located in Jackson, Wyoming.

Her original oil paintings command prices of $20,000 to $60,000 each. Affordable, limited-edition prints of her work are issued by Somerset House Publishing of Houston, Texas, and are available in galleries nationwide.

This lithograph of Glazier's "The Gathering Place" is 34 inches wide by 17 inches high; it is limited to an edition of 1,200 pieces. Her "Unbridled Spirit," left, is 34 inches wide by 17 inches high; it has been published by Somerset House in a limited edition of 1,200.

Adam Grimm

The youngest artist to win the Federal Duck Stamp competition, Adam Grimm was born in Elyria, Ohio, in 1978. "I used to draw for a few hours every day, even when I was very little. My mom liked it because it kept me out of trouble. I drew just about everything—comic book stuff, race cars and so forth. I got serious about drawing waterfowl when I was 13 and was encouraged to do it by my high school art teacher," says Grimm, who is also first Federal Duck Stamp contest winner to have placed in the Junior Duck Stamp Design Contest. Grimm had entered the junior contest twice—first during his sophomore year in high school, with a painting of a pintail, which took first place in the 1995 Ohio Federal Junior Duck Stamp Contest. He entered again in his junior year, when a painting of canvasbacks placed first in the Ohio contest and fourth in the National Junior Federal Duck Stamp Contest.

By the time he was in high school, Grimm knew that he wanted to spend his life as a wildlife artist. "I decided that I'd draw only what I wanted to draw, and if people didn't want to buy it, then I'd be a starving artist." That was not a popular attitude at Columbus College of Art and Design, where, he says, "realism was discouraged and wildlife art was considered a joke." Grimm studied there for about two years, often "butting heads" with his instructors, but never compromising. "They wanted us

The 2000 Alaska Duck Stamp features this 18-inch-wide by 13-inch-high oil on Masonite painting by Alan Grimm.

"Canvasback Pair" is 9 inches wide by 6½ inches high. A graphite on paper, "Golden Eagle," left, is 16 inches wide by 9 inches high.

to find ourselves, and find what we really wanted to do. I knew what I wanted to do. I wanted to win the Federal Duck Stamp competition."

Grimm's winning art, which appears on the 2000-01 stamp, features a mottled duck—one of two species that contest entrants were allowed to paint for the 1999 contest. (The other was the black scoder; it and the mottled duck were the only two species that had never been featured on a Federal Duck Stamp.) Grimm had never seen a mottled duck in the wild, so he spent a lot of time researching it. "Each species has its own personality, each carries itself differently," he notes. "There are so

many really neat kinds of waterfowl, and they all have different attitudes. I find that many people don't notice the animals and birds that are in nature until they see them in paintings. I hope my art makes people look closer at what is out there."

Upon winning the 1999 contest, Grimm decided to quit college in order to devote all of his time to painting. First, though, he spent a year touring the country, being honored for his winning art and, in turn, promoting the Federal Duck Stamp program. "When I look at the future and where I want to be, I feel that I have a long way to go. I'm really happy with what I've done so far, but I feel I'm supposed to do more," says Grimm, adding that he has a lot of ideas for future paintings. One painting that he did complete during his hectic year of travel was the commissioned artwork for the 2000 Alaska Duck Stamp. It features common eiders found on the shores of the 50th state. Limited-edition prints of Grimm's stamp art have been published by Steiner Prints, San Francisco, California.

Donald Heywood

Donald Heywood's first trip to Kenya changed his life and his art. The distinguished, award-winning British portrait artist—whose commissioned works include a life-size portrait of Queen Elizabeth II, a group portrait of 40 officers of the Household Cavalry and a portrait of King Goodwill Zwelithini, ka BhekuZulu, King of the Zulus—became fascinated with Africa and its wildlife. He now lives in Capetown, South Africa, and devotes his time to painting and preserving the animals that roam the Dark Continent. Heywood is a sponsor of Cheetah Conservation Fund and has a cheetah compound in his garden; he is also a patron of The Endangered Wildlife Fund and a founder member of Peace Parks Foundation 1997.

In addition to painting, Heywood has published two books. The first, *The Vanishing Faces of Southern Africa*, was released in 1994 and features his portraits of South Africans in traditional costumes. His second, *Wildlife Portraits*, is filled with both his paintings and drawings of Africa's animals; Heywood has donated the royalties from it to the World Wildlife Fund for Nature.

The artist is now involved in a major project with the Conservation & Research Center (CRC), part of the Smithsonian Institution's efforts to conserve the earth's biodiversity. CRC's scientists have helped preserve a variety of species, including the black-footed ferret, cheetah, Eld's dear, giant panda, clouded leopard and Hawaiian forest birds. Other CRC projects focus on saving habitats and restoring species to the wild. To raise funds for this important work, Heywood is creating 12 large-format drawings, each featuring a species that CRC's scientists have helped to preserve. These color drawings will be reproduced as limited-edition graphics. Individual prints will sell for $125 each; the portfolio of 12 will be available for $1,000. Production costs for the project are being paid by private and corporate sponsors, so all funds from the sale of the prints will be used for CRC's activities.

Born in Yorkshire, England, Heywood's artistic talent surfaced at an early age. When at the age of 12 he won a painting competition on BBC television, he was encouraged to pursue a career in the arts. He earned a B.A. degree from England's Leicester College of Art, and then taught at The London College of Printing, London, England. Meanwhile, his paintings were commanding ever-growing attention. He had exhibitions at London's prestigeous Tryon Gallery, DM Gallery and The Royal Academy; he also had an exhibition at Le Grand Palais Champs Elysees in Paris. In 1977, he was awarded a *Mention Honourable* by the Société des Artistes Francais.

Heywood believes that "there will always be an interest in wildlife art, but it must offer the collector something special and unique. If it can be linked to drawing attention to and fund-raising for endangered wildlife and conservation, then so much the better." In addition to raising considerable funds for wildlife conservation, Heywood's art provides unique portraits of animals. He describes his style as "extremely detailed, depending a lot on draughtsmanship. As with my portraits of people, I try with my wildlife art to portray individual animals and the character of the animal," he explains, adding: "In striving to portray the individual character in my work, I have taken as my influence the draughtsmanship of the more famous Renaissance artists, and have tried to develop this into a 20th-century technique. I feel my work is therefore very realistic, but following a 20th-century tradition." Heywood uses a variety of mediums, including pencil and oil paints. Prints of his work are available from Passion Publishing, located in Los Gatos, California.

Donald Heywood's "Leopard in Tree" has been issued by Passion Publishing as a Giclée on canvas, in a signed and numbered edition of 250, plus 25 artist proofs. It's 30 inches wide by 30 inches high.

Matthew Hillier

y earliest memories involve painting and animals," says Matthew Hillier. "I never painted anything else, it was always animals. I had a grandfather who painted animals in Wales, but I've never seen his work, and I have a cousin who paints animals professionally in England, though I do not know him well. My father was also artistic; he worked as a museum designer," adds Hillier, who was born in Farnham Common, about 30 miles from London, England, in 1958.

Hillier's talent was encouraged, and at age 16, he went to study at Dyfed College of Art, Carmarthen, West Wales—"the first college in England to specialize in wildlife illustration, as well as graphic design," he notes. He graduated with distinction at the age of 19, and began working as an illustrator. "I wanted to paint animals and make a living from painting animals. So at first, I did greeting cards and calendars, painting kittens and cuddly ducklings. Then I went into book illustration. I did the wildlife section of the *Guinness*

Book of Records for 15 years. I also did magazine covers and illustrated articles on wildlife." Another project was illustrating a monograph on rhinoceros. "I did nothing but paint rhinos for two years, and I loved it. I was lucky enough to go out to Africa and Sumatra, to study Sumatran rhinos in the wild. I was given a month to do each plate, and I got totally absorbed into watching and studying rhinos." When that project was completed, Hillier decided to concentrate on painting, rather than illustration. He was admitted into England's prestigious Society of Wildlife Artists, participated in Christie's wildlife art auctions, and he had one-man exhibitions throughout Great Britain. In 1995, he

won the World Wildlife Fund Fine Art Award.

"There is a thriving wildlife art scene in England," Hillier says, "so I didn't really think about the American scene. Then, by chance, an American agent turned up at my door and asked if he could take some of my work to the States." Soon after that, Hillier was invited to attend an American wildlife art show; more shows followed. Then he signed with Mill Pond Press, Venice,

Matthew Hillier's "Chinese Whispers—Rock-hopper Penguins," above, was selected for the Leigh Yawkey Woodson Art Museum's 2000 "Birds in Art" exhibition. His "Breaking the Silence—Egret," left, has been published by Mill Pond Press in a signed and numbered edition of 490, plus 39 artist proofs. The print is 21½ inches wide by 16 inches high."Sentinel," opposite page, is 16⅛ inches wide by 20 inches high. Hillier has been to Africa a number of times; for two years, on painting holidays, he taught art to local residents and tourists in Zimbabwe. "I enjoy teaching," says the artist. "It makes me go back to the basics and rethink how and why I do things."

Florida, to publish his work. "Living in England and coming here to do shows and work with an American publisher was very difficult logistically. My work got lost by freight companies, impounded by customs. Also, I wanted to familiarize myself with American wildlife," says the artist, who now resides in the United States.

One of the advantages of painting for Americans, Hillier says, is that he can do larger works. "The English tend to have smaller houses, so English paintings seem to be smaller." Another plus: "The artists here are very generous, talking about techniques, what paints and varnishes they use, ideas for paintings. I've enjoyed meeting the American artists and hanging out with them."

Hillier paints with acrylics on Masonite or clayboard, and describes his style as "representational," noting that American collectors seem to like a "slightly tighter approach than is popular in England. I love to do miniatures, which are very detailed," he says, "but I also enjoy doing large paintings, which are looser." Prices for his small paintings begin around $1,000; larger works sell for $16,000 to $24,000. The artist attends three major wildlife shows annually, and also makes a number of gallery appearances each year. He remains "passionate about rhinos," but is also attracted to painting big cats, herons and egrets—"graceful things that you can put into wonderful situations."

Matthew Hillier's "The Crossing" is 36 inches wide by 24 inches high. His "High Jinks," left, has been published in a signed and numbered edition of 450; it is 32½ inches wide by 16¼ inches high.

Mark Hopkins

Wildlife is just one of Mark Hopkins's subjects, but it is perhaps the most natural for him, as he's always loved the outdoors and its inhabitants. Also, he notes, "Wildlife presents an infinite variety of design possibilities, which satisfies my need for creativity. Along with that, I love the challenge of trying to convey the soul of an animal—the emotion and drama of the animal kingdom. I like to portray both the similarities and the differences between their world and mine."

Born in Atlanta, Georgia, in 1953, Hopkins has been interested in art for as long as he can remember. "I loved drawing as a kid, and when a teacher introduced me to wax sculpture, I knew I'd found what I wanted to do. I was fascinated by shapes and the way they fit together to become a three-dimensional image. I guess I never grew out of it."

He received a scholarship to the Atlanta College of Art, but the art courses there and elsewhere didn't satisfy him. "The anatomy courses were pretty helpful," he says, "but, other than that, they weren't teaching me things I wanted to learn. So I studied everything I could get my hands on, and learned by doing. Experience is an excellent teacher."

In order to support his six children, Hopkins was forced into a variety of jobs—including construction and janitorial services—but he always made time for creative endeavors. He experimented with various styles and media, eventually becoming an expert at the "lost wax" method of bronze casting, which he uses today to produce limited editions of his wax and clay originals.

Although many of his wildlife sculptures leave as much to the imagination as they portray, it is obvious that Hopkins has an intimate knowledge of his subjects. His company, Mark Hopkins Sculpture, Inc., is located in Rome, Georgia, but he now resides in Colorado. "Living at the base of the Rocky Mountains, I have quite a few opportunities to watch animals in their natural habitat," he says. "I often see eagles and hawks in my backyard. But since animals are not always available on demand, I also have a huge library of reference books and photos. Sometimes I work with taxidermists and their resource material, when I need to be sure of an anatomical detail."

The artist's sculptures are found in major corporate collections, as well as in the homes of the rich and famous, such as Bob Hope, Barbara Mandrell, Michael Jackson, Bart Starr, Clint Eastwood and former President George Bush. But Hopkins prides himself on producing bronze art that is available to people who thought they never could afford it. "Sculpture serves no essential useful function, so it's not a 'must have' for most of us. But what it can do is uplift and inspire us, and beautify our lives. By making bronze more affordable, I hope I have opened a door for many people to enrich their lives in a way they didn't think was possible," he says. His works sell for $300 to $19,000, but the average piece is $1,100.

"I often see eagles and hawks in my backyard," says Mark Hopkins, whose "Sovereign Territory" is shown here. It's 23 inches high and limited to an edition of 550.

"Rite of Passage," 30 inches high and 24 inches wide, is limited to an edition of 250. "Sculpture excites me, and I want others to experience the same thrill, both visually and emotionally," says Mark Hopkins. "With my wildlife, I want the viewer to enter the environment of the animal and feel a quiet reverence for nature."

Nancy Howe

The first woman to win the Federal Duck Stamp competition, Nancy Howe is a graduate of Vermont's Middlebury College, where she majored in art, but "didn't really get an art education." As she explains, "I didn't expect to have a career in art, so I didn't approach it that way." Also, she says, her painting style was "much more realistic than that of most artists and most art programs at the time, so I ended up doing a lot of independent study."

Howe was born in Summit, New Jersey, in 1950, and began painting as a youngster. "My dad set up an old drafting table for me, and throughout grade school and high school, I spent all my free time working at it. I painted just about every subject matter and with every medium you can imagine." The only rival to the drafting board was the countryside around Howe's home. "When I wasn't painting, I was outside building forts, slogging around in the swamps, and looking for salamanders and turtles."

While Howe continued to paint after college, she didn't pursue a career in art until the late 1980s, when her first marriage ended in divorce and she had two toddlers to support. "At that time, I really was untrained, but I was convinced I could make a go of it. A friend, who enjoyed hunting and was involved in Ducks Unlimited and other conservation programs, told me about the conservation stamp contests and urged me to enter them. That's what got me painting wildlife, although it was a natural evolution with the interests I had

"Nestled In," 23 inches wide by 18 inches high, has been published by Hadley House in a signed and numbered edition of 999.

"Higher Learning" is 26 inches wide by 42 inches high. "I usually select a subject because it has visual appeal or a strong design," says Howe. "But while painting, a thought or idea develops around that subject, so the painting becomes more than a depiction of the subject. It becomes an expression of an idea."

Howe's "Dust Storm" is 40 inches wide by 28 inches wide. "Sunday," left, is an oil on linen canvas; it is 36 inches wide by 24 inches high. Published by Hadley House, "Cygnature," opposite page, is 19 inches wide by 25 inches high. It is limited to an edition of 750 signed and numbered prints on paper, 75 artist proofs, and 75 signed and numbered canvas transfers.

in animals and the outdoors," she says.

Howe switched from acrylics to oils and began an intensive program of self-study. "I read how-to art books. I had a friend who had *American Artist* magazines dating back to the 1930s or so, and I went through all of them. When I found artists whose work I liked, I got books on them. I started going to museums, studying paintings and deciding what I liked." Throughout this time, she painted, developing a personal style that she describes as "subtle, with a soft, refined quality of realism that emphasizes light and strong design."

When Howe's painting of a king eider was selected for the 1991-92 Federal Duck Stamp, she gained a national reputation as a wildlife artist. She points out, however, that she also paints landscapes, still lifes, people. "My paintings usually begin with the selection of a subject that has visual appeal and strong design; but often, in the process of painting, a thought develops around the subject. By not having all the elements of the piece worked out in advance, I allow the painting to lead me. In this way, the success of the painting is not solely about creating an esthetic work; it is about the process of self discovery. Though I am primarily a studio painter," Howe adds, "reference for my work may include plein air and/or life studies, my own photos, or bird and animal specimens. The painting is often a synthesis of these supporting materials, combined with creative imagination."

Howe's work is exhibited at many wildlife and museum shows. She was the featured artist in the Bennington Center for the Arts' year 2000 "Art of the Animal Kingdom V" exhibition and national tour, and was one of 40 international artists chosen for the "Wildlife Art for the New Century" exhibit at the National Museum of Wildlife Art in Jackson, Wyoming. Prints of her work are published by Hadley House of Bloomington, Minnesota.

Terry Isaac

"When I was in grade school, I wanted to be an animator for Walt Disney," says Terry Isaac. Although his life took a different course, his childhood dream was realized in 1996, when the well-known wildlife artist was invited to paint the main character for Disney's *Dinosaur*, released in the spring of 2000. "Working on a movie is sort of magical," says Isaac, who painted a close up of Aladar's face and a full-body illustration, and served as a visual consultant for the film.

The Oregon artist is best known for his paintings of songbirds, although a wide variety of birds appear on his canvases, as do the large and small mammals of North America. His favorite subjects, though, are the blackcap chickadees, because they're "gregarious, friendly, fearless and have a nice song. They flock together in a group. They also have interesting colors and patterns—colors and patterns that go well with a variety of flowers," says

white picket fence in Matthew's yard, I was taken by their beauty," Isaac says. "The sun was shining brightly with the light shining through the flower petals. A purple-colored shadow was cast on the white fence. This reminded me of the effect of a stained-glass window being illuminated. Having never painted morning glories before, I was very excited about the possibility. With the yellow-gold center of the flowers, I thought a goldfinch would be the perfect bird to be a companion for the morning glories."

"On Eagles' Wings" is 36 inches wide by 24 inches high. "Morning Glories—American Goldfinch," right, is 9 inches wide by 17¾ inches high. Prints of Isaac's paintings are published by Mill Pond Press.

Isaac. "I often have flowers in my paintings. I have a lot of flowers in my yard, as well as flowering trees and bushes. I also have several bird feeders, so I get lots of birds."

Isaac's photo-realistic paintings are "a collage of bits and pieces," he says, explaining that they may be inspired by a photograph he's taken, but generally include elements from a variety of photos, as well as personal observations. For instance, he had the idea for his recent "Morning Glories—American Goldfinch" painting during a visit with fellow wildlife artist Matthew Hillier. "When I observed these morning glories growing up a

"King of the Mountain" is 45 inches wide by 24½ inches high. "For a long time, I had wanted to paint a majestic bull elk, but the right concept and scene eluded me," says Terry Isaac. "I had seen them many times, sometimes solitary and sometimes in a large herd. I had also wanted to paint this mountain scene for some time. Eventually I put two and two together. During the painting design process, I experimented with other subjects, but I kept returning to this bull elk—both subject and scene just seemed right together. The placement of the animal at the top of the rocky cliff truly makes him the 'king of the mountain' and gives him a vantage point from which he can survey his domain." Isaac's "Garden Tapestry—Mourning Dove," left, is 20 inches wide by 27½ inches high.

An admirer of Thomas Moran and Albert Bierstadt, who were experts at painting light, Isaac enjoys capturing the light that surrounds his subjects. Of course, he also pays great attention to depicting the characteristics that make the species unique and to accurately depicting their natural habitats. He generally uses acrylics for his works.

Isaac was born in Salem, Oregon, in 1958, and still lives in that city. He graduated with honors from Oregon College of Education (now Western Oregon University), located in Monmouth, and then taught junior high art for six years. He began painting full-time in 1987; the following year, Mill Pond Press, Venice, Florida, published prints of two of his paintings—one featuring a spotted owl, the other depicting timber wolves. Mill Pond Press continues to publish limited-edition prints of Isaac's work.

The artist has had his work featured in a number of shows, including "Birds in Art" exhibitions at the Leigh Yawkey Woodson Art Museum. He is the author of *Painting the Drama of Wildlife Step by Step*, and 14 of his waterfowl drawings appear in *Audubon Bird Handbook*, which was published in 1987.

Stephen Koury

"Most people are too busy to notice all of the cool little things going on all around them in nature, and with this a feeling of how precious and necessary the gift of nature is to all of us," says Stephen Koury, who hopes that his artwork will change this. "I try to tell stories, little and large, of the daily events going on in nature, in the most accurate and realistic way that I can," he explains. Large animals and birds are the lead characters in some of these stories, but more often than not, Koury's canvases star life's "little critters."

For instance, in his recent Little Jewels series of paintings, he focuses on "a square foot of nature and showing the intertwined goings-on—the visitors past and the current inhabitants, the texture and beauty of stones, earth and fallen leaves, as well as the vivid color of a resting butterfly." All are presented in an accurate, balanced and timeless manner. "Maybe, just maybe, these paintings will help people become just a little more aware of the little piece of earth they are standing on, and feel that everything in nature is connected," says the artist.

Born in Holbrook, Arizona, in 1957, Koury was the son of an art teacher who constantly urged him to paint what he saw, and gave him the materials and tips to do so. Painting took the back burner, though, when competing with sports and nature. "If I wasn't playing a sport, I was in the hills," Koury says. "I remember being stunned by the colors of a rainbow trout and wanting somehow to save those colors, or maybe the moment. I would spend hours watching animals and birds, following game trails, hunting for arrowheads and artifacts. I have always been moved by colors, shapes and textures, and the details of each and how nature presents an unlimited palette."

Koury earned an A.S. degree at Central Arizona College, and B.S. and M.S. degrees at the University of Wyoming, Laramie. He spent eight years as a college baseball coach, first at his alma mater, then at Florida Southern College in Lakeland, Florida, where he and his wife, Necia, now live. "Our lifestyle is all encompassing," he says. "For Necia and me, the wonder and desire to be out in nature is always there. The things we do and the places we visit go into each painting. We grow flowers and garden for butterflies and hummingbirds, as well as the little critters that come along. We feed birds and enjoy birding. We like to travel and enjoy watching animals and studying their environment. Photography is a big part of our life, and we still like hiking and looking for arrowheads, fossils and cool rocks."

Koury, who paints with gouache and acrylic, is a

Stephen Koury's "Painted Jewel" is 8¼ inches wide by 9⅝ inches high. It has been published in a signed and numbered edition of 500. "Yin & Yang," opposite page, is 11½ inches wide by 6 inches high. The first issue in Stephen Koury's Little Jewels series, it has been published in a signed and numbered edition of 500.

member of the Society of Animal Artists. He was honored by Florida Ducks Unlimited as its 1991 and 1992 Artist of the Year, and its Sponsor Print Artist in 1996. He won the People's Choice Award at the 1995-96 Southern Wildlife Festival. He was the U.S. Forestry Service National Poster Artist in 1996 and the 1996 Quail Unlimited National Poster Artist. He was the 1997-98 Florida State Turkey Stamp contest winner. He was the Millennium Featured Artist at Florida Wildlife Expo 2000, and has had his work featured in a number of national magazines, including *U.S. Art*, *Wildlife Art* and *Collector Editions*. Prices for the artist's originals begin at $650; prints of his work are available from his company, Koury Wildlife Art, Lakeland, Florida.

Not all of Koury's paintings are of little critters. Inspired by a trip to Africa, "Gold Dust" is 28 inches wide by 18 inches high. It has been published in an edition of 85 Giclées. "Quail Cover," left, is nine inches wide by six inches high. Part of the artist's Little Jewels series, it has been published in a signed and numbered edition of 500. Two more of Koury's Little Jewel paintings are shown on the opposite page. The upper painting, titled "Landing Pad," is 8½ inches wide by 5½ inches high. Below it is "Natural Cameo," nine inches wide by seven inches high. They have been published in signed and numbered editions of 500 each.

Lee Kromschroeder

When I was a kid in San Diego," says Lee Kromschroeder, who was born there in 1951, "I'd write a note to my mom saying 'going out exploring.' Then I'd take a peanut butter and jelly sandwich and a jar of milk, and wander off ten miles into the back country. I remember how I loved to get down into a river valley and get completely soaked wading up the river." Kromschroeder also loved the beach. "I'm a surfer," he says, "a body surfer and scuba diver. I got certified in 1969—I was one of the early scuba divers out here in California. What an amazing place it is under the sea." Another favorite haunt was the San Diego Zoo. "I was fascinated by the animals there, without ever realizing that they would become such a part of my life's work."

Kromschroeder's father was a dentist. His mother, grandmother and several aunts were artists. "When I was in grade school, my mother would take me to my grandmother's house on weekends. There, instead of doing the little pencil drawings that I did in school when I was supposed to be doing my math, I got to paint with her *oil* paints. By the time I was in seventh grade, I was attending adult painting classes at the community center. One day I looked around and thought, 'I paint better than all these grown ups.'" This was quite a revelation for Kromschroeder, as he'd always been tagged a "slow learner." Indeed, he did have difficulty in school, but not from lack of intelligence; Kromschroeder is dyslexic.

"I realized I had to be an artist," he says, "when my

high school counselor told me to go surfing in Mexico after graduation, because I'd never get into college." He did get into college, though, and graduated cum laude from San Francisco State University. "Because I'm a such a slow reader, I had to work my tail off, but the ironic thing is that I ended up getting almost straight A's." While a degree in painting and printmaking doesn't guarantee success—or even a job—Kromschroeder praises his college experience for having made him a more well-rounded person and for giving him a solid grounding in art history.

Kromschroeder's first job was doing manual labor for an auction house. Then one day, his boss saw one of his paintings and asked him to paint a Western scene. "When he agreed to pay me $500 for it, I began hustling," the artist says with a laugh. He accepted private commissions and also did product design work for large companies. In his spare time, he did nude studies. What paid the bills, though, were his landscapes. "At some point, I decided to put animals in my landscapes. I began doing just animals in their environment in 1978, and I've sold everything I've painted since then." He's also garnered his share of awards and honors, and had more than 40 of his paintings published as limited-edition prints by Wild Wings, Lake City, Minnesota.

Now married and the father of two, Kromschroeder continues to live in the San Diego area, but he travels the world to research the wildlife he paints. While he loves the travel, he bemoans what is happening to the environment here in the United States and abroad. "I feel like wildlife art is a cataloging of the world before man's supremacy and destruction of it. I fear I'm cataloging things that are going to disappear soon."

Lee Kromschroeder's "Pandemonium—Lion" is 30 inches wide by 15 inches high. It has been published by Wild Wings in an edition of 750. "Vertical Rise—Orcas," right, has been published in an edition of 950. It is 11 inches wide by 31¼ inches high. "There are a million ways a wildlife artist can make a mistake," says Kromschroeder, which is why field work is so essential. "When I put a plant in a scene, I don't have to ask, 'is that plant indigenous?' I was there, I've seen that place, I've photographed it." He's also familiar with many sea creatures, as he's been scuba diving since the late 1960s.

Art LaMay

When I try to think of what birds I haven't yet painted, I can't come up with any. I've even done vultures," says Art LaMay. As to his personal favorite—and a favorite of his many collectors—it's the great blue heron. "This is *my* bird," says the artist. "I've studied this bird for more than 25 years. I've painted it in every posture imaginable. I guess I like it because of its majesty and its sheer beauty."

LaMay was born in Jersey City, New Jersey, in 1938, but was raised in York, Pennsylvania, where his family moved when he was in grade school. "I've always had a

desire to paint, and when in my teens, I was influenced by the work of well-known wildlife artists," says LaMay, who received his formal art training at York Academy of Arts. "Also, for as long as I can remember, I have had a special fascination with nature. To know that I have captured the subject of the scene as it really is in its natural setting is a true encouragement. To do a portrait-type picture, to bring out birds' comical or even human characteristics as we often see them is true enjoyment," he adds.

Early in LaMay's career, he used oils and painted a variety of wildlife—animals as well as birds. Then, some two decades years ago, he switched to watercolors and limited his subject to "anything that flies." He calls himself a "portrait painter" of wildlife, explaining, "I use very little background. I take a simple, high-definition, realistic approach." His expertise at this approach has earned him a place in *Who's Who in Wildfowl Art*—a listing of the top 100 artists in the field, as well as national recognition. LaMay was honored as the 1986 Southeastern Wildlife Artist of the Year, the 1987 Northeastern Wildlife Artist of the Year, the 1991 Northern Wildlife Artist of the Year, and the 1995-96 Ducks Unlimited International Wildlife Artist of the Year. He was the 1989 Virginia State Duck Stamp artist, and in 1992 was inducted into the Easton, Maryland, Waterfowl Festival's National Hall of Fame. That same year, a gallery at the famous Ward Museum in Salisbury, Maryland, was named for him. One of his paintings was selected by the National Wild Turkey Federation for its 1998-99 print, and another became the National Rifle Association's 1998-99 Print of the Year.

LaMay's originals sell for $1,500 to $8,500 each. He publishes his own prints, which are available in galleries nationwide. His artwork is also found on a variety of usable products, including steins issued by Anheiser-Busch, dinnerware produced by Big Sky Carvers, T-shirts from M.R. Ducks and popcorn cans from Olive Can Company. His paintings have also appeared on Christmas cards issued by National Wildlife, Ducks Unlimited and the National Rifle Association.

The artist and his wife moved to Florida about

Art LaMay's "Blue Winged Warbler on Iris" is 24 inches wide by 30 inches high.

"Widgeon Flight" is 30 inches wide by 48 inches high. LaMay's watercolors are simple, yet factual, and have "a whimsical approach that gives my clientele a good feeling," he says.

15 years ago, but he's far from retired. In fact, he complains about having little free time. He does, however, get away from his easel for an occasional day of fishing and, he readily admits, "I still get a thrill birdwatching, even if the bird I'm watching is a lowly sparrow." Fans of LaMay's art can usually find him at three annual shows: the Southeastern Wildlife Exposition, held in Charleston, South Carolina; the Florida Wildlife Festival, held in Lakeland, Florida; and Easton Waterfowl Festival, held each November in Easton, Maryland. In addition, LaMay is a regular guest artist at Epcot's annual Flowers and Garden Show.

Jim Lamb

"Wildlife and landscapes have interested me for as long as I can remember," says Jim Lamb, who was born in Hamilton, Montana, in 1946. Fishing with his dad, hunting and hiking filled his youth. Trips to wilderness areas, zoos and game reserves are now enjoyable pastimes, as he researches the wildlife he paints. Also helpful are visits to natural history museums and with people who rehabilitate wild animals that have been injured. Then there are the rewards of doing plein-air paintings—small works Lamb does in oils directly from nature.

While doing these paintings, Lamb says, "I often see wildlife of all kinds, because I am quiet, move relatively slowly, and am there in their world long enough for them to get used to my presence. One time while painting in the Tetons, I had the sense I was being watched. I finally stopped painting and looked around. Not 50 yards away was a large moose, staring at me from a small grove of aspen trees. I had no idea how long I had been observed, but I have a hunch the moose was not the only curious resident in the neighborhood who had noticed me."

Lamb studied at the Art Center College of Design in Los Angeles, and spent 15 years as a free-lance illustrator, working for advertising agencies, corporations and organizations such as The Smithsonian Institution, The White House, the National Football League, NASA and The Jet Propulsion Laboratory. He's also designed stamps for the US Postal Service. He considers himself a "good" illustrator, but believes his best work "has always in some way been connected to my own experiences in nature." The things that excite his creative instincts, Lamb says, "can be as simple as a warm evening light at the top of a tree, or a patch of snow that takes on an interesting shape. These simplicities strike my fancy, and I feel the need to somehow express them with a brush and some paint. Having done that, I suppose my

"Ridge Runner," left, is an acrylic on board; it is 11 inches wide by 15 inches high. "Repetitions," depicting a black-crowned night heron at water's edge, is an original oil on board. It is 30 inches wide by 15 inches high. "Secret Passage," oposite page, depicts trumpeter swans. Published by Wild Wings in an edition of 750, it is 36 inches wide by 28 inches high. (Photo of artist: Kristi Lamb)

only concern is that others respond with some of the same appreciation I had for the subject when I was first touched by it myself. Sometimes I feel I succeed in reaching that end, other times I may fail, but nevertheless, those remain my goals each time I set out to create a piece of artwork.

"The more time I spend outdoors studying and painting from nature," Lamb says, "the more I am impressed with the infinite creativity of the Master Artist in His use of design, color, light, texture and shapes. I have a lot to learn from His work and not much time to learn it."

In addition to wildlife, Lamb paints landscapes and puppies. "The puppies and the wildlife are rendered relatively tightly," he says, because print and plate collectors seem to prefer "extreme realism. For me, this can

"A Canada Morning," issued in a print edition of 700, is 24 inches wide by 10½ inches high. "Elegance in White," opposite page, featuring trumpeter swans in sunlight, is 17 inches wide by 30 inches high. Wild Wings has published it in an edition of 1,000.

become tedious at times, and in recent years I have developed a very different style for my landscape oils. Painting on location has caused me to 'loosen up' a great deal, so these paintings, which are primarily for galleries, are more 'painterly' or 'impressionistic' in style, though still very much classified as 'realism.'" Lamb's oils sell for $650 to $12,000 each. Prints of his paintings are published by Wild Wings, Lake City, Minnesota. His work has also been featured on collector plates that were produced by The Hamilton Collection of Jacksonville, Florida.

Mark Everett Larson

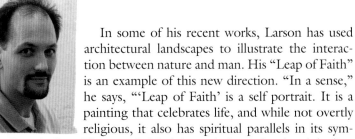

"I grew up hunting and fishing with my father, which fueled my fascination with wildlife," says Mark Everett Larson, who was born in Portland, Oregon, in 1964. When on his own, young Larson would often "put on my waders, sling duck decoys over my shoulder, hop on my bike and ride to a nearby marsh, just so I could sneak up on ducks and observe them up close." Getting up close and personal with wildlife is still the artist's idea of a good time. For example, after a recent one-man show in Fairbanks, Alaska, he treated himself to "three days hiking in Denali National Park, watching grizzlies and being chased by moose. What fun!"

Larson's interest in art developed at an early age, too. "I have been drawing and painting, usually animals, since I was three years old. Even when I thought I might do something else—I have an accounting degree, in addition to my art degree from Portland State University—I could not escape the fact that I was born to be an artist," he says. Fortunate to have had his talent encouraged, Larson is committed to assisting today's young artists and enjoys being a guest speaker at schools, where he shares his own experiences and expertise. He is also committed to wildlife conservation, working with groups such as Ducks

In some of his recent works, Larson has used architectural landscapes to illustrate the interaction between nature and man. His "Leap of Faith" is an example of this new direction. "In a sense," he says, "'Leap of Faith' is a self portrait. It is a painting that celebrates life, and while not overtly religious, it also has spiritual parallels in its symbolism. The cross behind the rock dove's head and the lion on the ceiling are both references to the strength and glory of God. For me personally, the lion is also a symbol of personal victory and triumph. The dove facing away in the

"Solitary Dawn—Moose," an oil on linen, is 40 inches wide by 24 inches high. "Leap of Faith," left, is an oil and gold leaf on panel; it is 24 inches wide by 41½ inches high. Inspired by a 1999 trip to Florence, Italy, it is one of Larson's new architectural landscapes that illustrate the interaction between nature and man. "Moonlight Crossing—Grizzlies," opposite page, is 24 inches wide by 30 inches high; it's been published on canvas and as a Giclée. Larson saw this grizzly at Alaska's Denali National Park. "I was attracted to the abstract shape of light on the bear's face, and was reminded of Rembrandt, who was able to convey so much character with so little, often throwing a subject in deep shadow while highlighting just a little of the face. I attempted to do that with this painting, which was difficult because I had to imagine this scene at night and convert all my daytime references to night," he says.

shadows in the upper right is a reference to my life before I was an artist, and the partial self-portrait at the bottom, while purposefully vague and mysterious, adds a meaningful human element to the painting and helps tie it to the present."

Larson generally paints with oils on canvas, Masonite or copper plate. His originals sell for $300 to $10,000 each. He regularly exhibits at wildlife shows, especially those held in the Pacific Northwest, where he continues to live, and in Alaska. In 1994 Larson was named Alaska Ducks Unlimited Artist of the Year and was the Featured Artist at the House of Wood Gallery in Fairbanks. In 1999, he was the Featured Artist at Fairbank's New Horizons Gallery.

Unlimited, Trout Unlimited, Clark Skamania Flyfishers and the Rocky Mountain Elk Foundation.

Larson calls his painting style "abstracted realism," explaining, "I use abstract shapes to integrate an animal into its environment, giving it a sense of place." His innovative style bridges the gap between traditional, realistic wildlife paintings and modern art. By pushing the boundaries of wildlife art, Larson hopes it will become "a more visible, viable and vital art form."

David A. Maass

Few wildlife artists begin their professional careers as jewelry designers. Nor do they begin painting while in the Marines. But that's the background of one of today's top wildfowl artists, David A. Maass. Although he was drawing battleships, cowboys and Indians when he was just three and four years old—"All kids draw a bit," he says—his artistic journey began in high school, when he served on the committee that was responsible for selecting the class ring. "We took a trip to Josten's, which makes the majority of class rings in this country, as well as rings for West Point, Annapolis, the Super Bowl and the World Series, and I was fascinated by their art and design department. So I applied for a job with them right after I graduated from high school." Because he didn't have any formal art training, he could only get a job in the company's tool and dye department. But he was told it would give him a good mechanical background for advancing into design, and, he says, "It did." Maass not only moved into the design department, he ended up heading it before leaving the company in the mid 1960s in order to paint full-time.

As for the Marines, his job at Josten's was interrupted for two years while he did his mandatory military service. "When I was living off base," Maass says, "I missed my native Minnesota. So I started drawing and sketching the wildlife that I had been interested in back home. And that led to my painting." It was, perhaps, inevitable—certainly fortuitous—that young Maass became interested in wildlife, as his mother and step-father, he says, "were real outdoors people. My mother won the

"Merrymeeting Bay—Black Ducks" is 36 inches wide by 22 inches high. It has been published by Wild Wings in a limited edition of 450. "Working the Ledges—Eiders," opposite page, is 33 inches wide by 22 inches high. It has been published in a limited edition of 95. Maass often takes photos for background reference; both of these painting are set in Maine, near Brunswick, where the artist's stepson attended college.

Minnesota State Trapshooting Championship back in the early days; my step-father was also very active in trap-shooting and target shooting and hunting. Being brought up by a couple of hunters, and having always loved to draw, made it just natural that I would get into wildlife painting," he adds.

Maass was selling his original art in galleries when he was in his mid twenties; he began painting full-time about ten years later, and hasn't stopped. About his style, he says: "I use a lot of paint when I paint. If you get up close and study my paintings, you'll see that they're not as detailed as they look. But when somebody stands back and looks at them, I want them to be able to say, 'That's the way it looks to me when I'm out there.' There's detail in my work, but I don't try to paint every feather, every blade of grass," Maass explains. His primary subjects are North American birds—"mostly game birds," he says. "A lot of my research is done while I'm hunting, although I do research when it's not hunting season, too." Like many wildlife artists, he takes a lot of photos, but he uses his primarily for reference when painting his backgrounds.

Over the years, he's won 33 duck and conservation stamp competitions, including two Federal Duck Stamp Contests. The 1974 Federal Duck Stamp features his painting of eiders; the 1982, his painting of canvasbacks. He's had three books of his art published (the most recent is *Wildfowl of North America*), was honored by *U.S. Art* magazine in 1997 with the title of Master Artist, has had more than 300 of his paintings published by Wild Wings as limited-edition prints, and has had his art featured on plates and other collectibles from The Danbury Mint. Also, his work has graced Brown & Bigelow calendars for more than 30 years.

The artist currently lives on the outskirts of Minneapolis, on land adjacent to a lake and woods, where there is an abundance of wildfowl to inspire future paintings. "I feel like I'm the luckiest person in the world to be able to do what I've always wanted to do and make a living at it. And I never really have to retire," he adds. While Maass has done more than 50 paintings a year, he now does just 15 or 16 paintings annually, with six of them for the Brown & Bigelow calendars.

Maass has supported wildlife conservation efforts throughout his career. His donations of paintings and prints have raised millions for groups such as Ducks Unlimited, the National Wild Turkey Federation and the Ruffed Grouse Society. More recently, he's become involved with the Delta Waterfowl Foundation; based near Winnipeg, Canada, this organization has research and educational programs.

Tom Mansanarez

One of four artistic sons of artist Manuel Mansanarez, Tom Mansanarez believes that his artistic abilities may well have been inherited, but notes that it is "a deep love of wildlife and horses that gave me the subject matter to express this gift. Being an artist is what I *am*," he says, "not what I've become. A deep love of the outdoors and a father that took us camping and hunting and fishing is what inspired me to document wildlife. The sheer diversity of wildlife around the world is another driving force. There's always another animal I'd like to paint," he notes.

Mansanarez has had no formal art training, but informal tutoring and growing up in an artistic family played a role in developing his talent. Also, workshops with some of America's top artists—including Robert Bateman,

John Seerey-Lester and Tucker Smith—helped him hone his skills. He describes his style as "realistic, but not photo-realism. I want the viewer to see and feel the paint up close, yet have a tight, realistic feel from a few feet away," he explains. "I paint wild encounters, and I want to put the viewer into the moment of interaction, to have the viewer feel the tension or joy or peacefulness of wildlife in its day-to-day routines." His original oils on canvas or linen sell for $2,000 to $15,000 each. Prints of his work are issued by Cattle Creek Publishing, North Logan, Utah.

A native of California—Mansanarez was born in San Bernadino in 1962—the artist now lives with his wife and two daughters in Idaho Falls, Idaho. He has painted a variety of wildlife over the years, but currently concentrates on North American animals, many of which live in Yellowstone and the Grand Teton National Parks, which are near his home. Like his fellow wildlife artists, Mansanarez finds time in the field invaluable. "Personal contact, handling, sketching and photographing a specific animal is the best way to capture its personality," he says. Such research can be dangerous, but as Mansanarez discovered, it has its comic side, too. "During a research trip in Yellowstone with some other artists," he relates, "we found a lovesick, rutting bull moose with one cow. He was chasing two smaller bulls away from his cow when I showed up. I was wearing a cowboy hat that he apparently mistook for horns, as he singled me out to chase away. He wouldn't leave me alone until I took off my hat!"

The artist has contributed to many wildlife organizations over the years, because "I want my children's children to enjoy the experiences I've had." Mansanarez cites Ducks Unlimited as "a perfect example of what can be done to ensure this. It has turned around the declining wetlands, and duck and goose populations, to what are now some all-time record numbers of geese and ducks."

Mansanarez's paintings have helped call attention to the continuing need for this type of work. For example, they has been chosen for seven Canadian Conservation Stamps. Also, he was honored as the 1992 and 1998 Artist of the Year by the Foundation of North American Sheep; he was the Mule Deer Foundation's 1997 Artist of the Year; and he was twice chosen for the Masters Collectors Series by the Rocky Mountain Elk Foundation.

Tom Mansanarez's painting of a coyote, titled "Mousin' Around," left, was featured on the 1995 Nova Scotia Conservation Stamp. The original oil, 24 inches wide by 18 inches high, has been published in a limited edition of 950 prints on paper. Featuring a bobcat and squirrel, "Out on a Limb," opposite page, is 24 inches wide by 18 inches high; it has been reproduced as a print on paper or canvas. "Cats are very interesting to me," says the artist, "because of their sheer beauty and the challenge of capturing their silent, stalking stealth. Also, their eyes are deep and inviting, almost a calling sign of their wildness. The essence of a wildcat is almost indefinable, but I try to define it in my art." An oil on linen, "Risky Business," right, is 36 inches wide by 24 inches high. Available as a print on paper or canvas, it is limited to an edition of 750, plus 95 artist proofs.

Carl McCleskey

In 1984, Carl McCleskey decided to "go on sabbatical," to leave the Atlanta, Georgia, area where he lived and worked as a mechanical engineer and move to Lookout Mountain. There, he and his wife, Betsy Scott, built their own home. Once it was completed, McCleskey realized he needed something to do, so he began "playing around with sculpture." His mother-in-law was impressed with his pieces, and encouraged him. Then he met another sculptor who worked in bronze and had his own foundry. This man offered to let McCleskey cast his work in the foundry, so he began creating bronzes. When he took them to wildlife shows, they quickly sold. Today, because much of McCleskey's work is done on commission, he regularly attends just two wildlife shows a year. One of them is the Southeastern Wildlife Art Show held in Charleston, South Carolina, which McCleskey calls "one of the largest and finest wildlife shows in the world." The other is the Plantation Wildlife Art Show, held annually in Thomasville, Georgia.

McCleskey was born in 1935 and raised in the countryside surrounding Marietta, Georgia. "My father was a self-taught engineer and was very talented with his hands. He was always making things or drawing. I enjoyed watching him, helping him at times," says McCleskey, who credits his father with inspiring his own artistic endeavors. The other thing he enjoyed as a lad was

"Water Dance," 42 inches high, is a life-size bronze issued in an edition of eight. Carl McCleskey admires river otters because of their efficiency and playfulness.

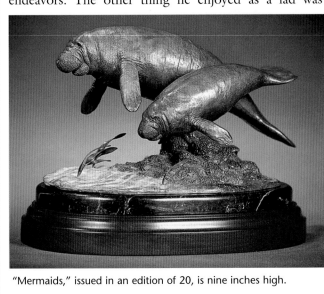

"Mermaids," issued in an edition of 20, is nine inches high.

exploring Georgia's fields, streams and swamps; through his wanderings, he gained an intimate knowledge of and appreciation for the diversity of the natural world.

The artist hopes his work will "open a window in people's minds that will let them see that all animals, including those that are feared or considered ugly, have their place and in their own way are beautiful." As a conservationist and member of Nature Conservancy and Bat Conservancy, McCleskey also hopes that his work will help call attention to what we have to lose if our wildlife isn't protected. "Every extinction makes the world a poorer place to live," he notes. One of the artist's hands-on conservation efforts, on which he's spent a great deal of time and money, is reclaiming an abandoned strip mine.

"Lowland Gorilla Family," sculpted by McCleskey and his wife, Betsy Scott, is limited to an edition of six. It is 42 inches high and six feet wide. The first piece in this edition is on display at The Audubon Institute in New Orleans. "Asian Rhinos," left, was issued in an edition of 20. It is ten inches high, 21 inches long and ten inches wide.

McCleskey's bronzes, which capture an animal in the middle of an ordinary act, have a fluidity that makes one aware of the animals' inherent power and grace. Occasionally, the artist also shares his subjects' playful natures. This is particularly true of his pieces depicting river otters, which are among his favorite animals. "Their love of life and intelligence allow them to make the most of everything," he says. "They live in water, fish for a living, and are so efficient that they have ample time for play and relaxation. What more could anyone ask? If there is such a thing as reincarna-tion, I would hope to return as an otter."

Prices for McCleskey's bronzes begin at $300 and go up to $50,000. Most of the costly, life-size or larg-er pieces are commissioned works that the artist has created with his wife, Betsy Scott. A number of their joint creations, including sculptures of gorillas, a chee-tah and a gazelle, can be found in The Audubon Institute in New Orleans, Louisianna. Two monumen-tal lions that will flank the front gate into New Orleans' Audubon Park were also created by the husband-and-wife team.

Bruce Miller

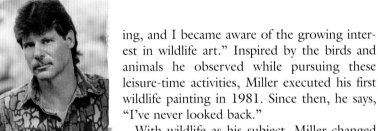

When he was four years old, Bruce Miller was drawing people. When he was in second grade, he won his first art contest. When he was in seventh grade, he began painting with acrylics. Then, at age 36, the Minneapolis-born artist won his first national contest: the Michigan Wildlife Art Festival's 1988 Artist of the Year competition. More awards and honors followed. He was the 1991 Minnesota Deerhunters Association Artist of the Year, the 1993 Wildlife & Western Art Show Artist of the Year, the 1997 Minnesota Heritage Foundation Artist of the Year, and the 1999 Ducks Unlimited International Artist of the Year. His work won seven state conservation stamp contests, plus the 1993-94 Federal Duck Stamp Contest and the

ing, and I became aware of the growing interest in wildlife art." Inspired by the birds and animals he observed while pursuing these leisure-time activities, Miller executed his first wildlife painting in 1981. Since then, he says, "I've never looked back."

With wildlife as his subject, Miller changed his style. "My work from 1982 to the present time is realism, primarily painted in acrylics. Many of my current oil paintings are impressionistic realism," he says. "Using atmospheric mood and/or strong lighting, I attempt to elicit emotion in all of my paintings. From feelings of peacefulness to dramatic impact, emotions are always part of a successful painting," he says.

Miller, now "a fanatical fly fisherman and bird/waterfowl hunter," gets many of his ideas during mornings spent in the marsh or evenings on the trout stream. "These hobbies allow me to enjoy nature during the magical 'low-light' times of the day," he explains. He does not, however, use time spent hunting and fishing as substitutes for serious research and animal watching. "The best part of my job is doing research on location," Miller notes. "I take all of my own reference photographs, and don't paint any birds or animals that I have not seen in the wild. This includes my African works."

Like many wildlife artists, as well as avid hunters and fishermen, Miller is concerned about the survival of our world's wild-

1999 Ducks Unlimited competition. Prints of his paintings are published by Hadley House, Bloomington, Minnesota.

Although Miller spent a year as an art major at Minnesota's St. Cloud University, he developed his style and technique through self study and experimentation. After graduating from high school, he went to Europe and visited major museum collections there. Then, after leaving St. Cloud University, he put in long nights and weekends experimenting with style and subject matter, while supporting himself by working as a building contractor. "In the late 1970s," he says, "I was doing abstract paintings. But then I developed an interest in hunting and fish-

life. To help ensure that it is here for future generations, he donates to numerous conservation organizations, including Ducks Unlimited, Pheasants Forever, Rocky Mountain Elk Foundation, Minnesota Waterfowl Association and Trout Unlimited. He continues to live in Minnesota, sharing a home on one of the state's more than 10,000 lakes with his wife, Deb, and their two children.

"Loon Point" is 28 inches wide by 16¾ inches wide. Hadley House has published it in a signed and numbered edition of 950. "The Challenger," opposite page, has been published by Hadley House in a signed and numbered edition of 750. It is 18 inches wide by 24 inches high. Trips to Yellowstone National Park provide inspiration for many of Miller's paintings of elk.

John Mullane

I don't have to go to Africa to be inspired. I get inspired just by opening my front door. I paint the ordinary things that are really extraordinary to me," says John Mullane, who was born in the Bronx in 1964 and still lives in that much-maligned New York City borough. "I have my favorite little spots at the botanical gardens, and there are places in Westchester and Upstate New York that I just love. Central Park is wonderful, too. I go to the Museum of Natural History to study the animals and skins there. As a kid I haunted the Bronx Zoo, and I still go there frequently to research animals."

As a youngster, Mullane had two passions: art and music. He began drawing when he was about four; he began playing drums at age fourteen. When it came time to choose a career, the musical artist thought it would be neat to be a

"The Only Game in Town," above, has been published by Mill Pond Press in a signed and numbered edition of 450. The print is 22 inches wide by 11 inches high. "Autumn Afternoon," 29⅜ inches wide by 19⅛ inches high, has been published in a signed and numbered edition of 650. "I drove hundreds of miles into Pennsylvania looking for the perfect tree for this painting, one with leaves in nice fall colors," says John Mullane. "I came home, went to the Bronx Zoo, and found just the tree I've been looking for—it was right here in my own backyard."

movie poster artist. He enrolled in The Fashion Institute of Technology and studied general illustration for three years. Then, in the late 1980s, he discovered *The Art of Robert Bateman*. "That book totally changed my life, or at least the direction of my art," he says. "I had always been interested in animals and wildlife, but I didn't realize that people were painting like Bateman was and actually making a living out of it."

Mullane quit school and got a night job as a doorman, so he could do field work and paint in the daytime. He also was playing drums in his band, "The Raw Poets." Married and with two children, Mullane paid a price to paint. "I'd get up, spend some time with the kids, paint, go do a gig, go to my doorman's job, unload the drums into the lobby, do my job, reload the drums, haul them home, go to sleep, and then begin the cycle again." The first reward for this grueling schedule came in 1992, when his "Baby Jay" painting was accepted into the Leigh Yawkey Woodson Art Museum's "Birds in Art" exhibition. Other exhibits fol-

lowed, as did sales of his paintings.

Mullane was able to quit his job as a doorman, but it wasn't until the late 1990s that he also put aside his career as a drummer. "Once I really focused on my art, things started to happen," he says. "For instance, a representative of Mill Pond Press saw my work at Terry Isaac's 1999 show, and offered to publish prints of my paintings. Most of my idols are signed with Mill Pond—I still have to pinch myself at times. I mean, I'm hanging out with Bateman and Terry Isaac and Rod Frederick, Dan Smith and Matthew Hellier. These guys are my friends now, and they're so inspiring to be around."

One of Mullane's paintings was accepted for Leigh Yawkey Woodson's 2000 exhibition, and he gets a lot of commissions for paintings of North American birds and mammals. "I use mostly acrylic, but also gouache and watercolor," he says. "I often do extensive pencil drawings, and sometimes loose watercolor studies, before beginning on a painting. My paintings are realistic, but I don't copy a photograph. Rather, I use photos as pieces in a puzzle that I put together." It's usually an animal that inspires his work—a squirrel, raccoon, songbird. "Then I try to find an appropriate setting for it. That's the fun part," he adds, "going out and searching for the perfect setting or scene."

Roy Benjiman Nauffts

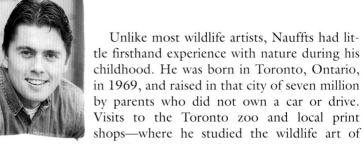

I truly believe I was born with the talent to reproduce anything I see," says Roy Benjiman Nauffts, who earned the nickname "the artist" when he was in grade school. His early artistic subjects were hockey stars and comic book characters. "When I was in my early teens, I became intrigued by television shows about wildlife, such as Jacques Cousteau's *Underwater Kingdom* and Mutual of Omaha's *Wild Kingdom.* Then, when I was about 18, I saw a painting by Robert Bateman, and I knew I wanted to spend my life painting wildlife."

Unlike most wildlife artists, Nauffts had little firsthand experience with nature during his childhood. He was born in Toronto, Ontario, in 1969, and raised in that city of seven million by parents who did not own a car or drive. Visits to the Toronto zoo and local print shops—where he studied the wildlife art of others—served as substitutes for trekking the countryside. He did, however, get rare trips to a friend's cabin on a northern Canadian lake; recalling those times, he says, "I never wanted to be anywhere else."

When he was high school age, his mother encour-

"High Country Cougar," an acrylic on Masonite, has been published in a limited edition of 1,150 prints. It is 30 inches wide by 20 inches high. "Autumn Red-Tail," opposite page, is 30 inches wide by 24 inches high. Roy Benjiman Nauffts has published it in a limited edition of 1,150.

aged him to apply for the specialty art program at Danforth Technical School in Toronto. "I made the grade and was rewarded with four of my eight courses being art classes," he says. "Unfortunately, having a child at the age of 16 forced me to leave school and seek full-time employment to support my family." He earned his high school diploma through a correspondence course. He then took art classes at the famous Sheridan College, in Oakville, Ontario, and computer design courses at Toronto's Desktop Publishing Associates.

Nauffts began drawing wildlife when he was in his early twenties, and quickly turned to painting with acrylics on Masonite. He still enjoys going to the Toronto zoo, where he researches his subjects, but zoo visits no longer take the place of field trips to study animals in the wild. In fact, he now spends considerably more time sketching and photographing birds and animals in their natural environments than he does painting in his studio.

North American birds and animals are the artist's primary subjects, with the grizzly being one of his favorites. "Its power is very exhilarating and its beautiful coat is always challenging and rewarding to paint," he says. His originals, available in Toronto galleries, sell for $850 to $6,500; prints of his work, which he began publishing in 1999, are also available.

In discussing wildlife art, Nauffts says Canadians' interest in the genre has flourished over the past five or ten years, and he believes it will become even more in demand in the future. "As more cement is poured over grassy fields, and more tall trees are replaced with tall buildings, more people will seek out a little bit of peace and tranquillity, and what easier way to attain it than through wildlife art. This is one of the reasons my own home is filled with wildlife paintings and sculpture— they bring the peace of the wilderness into the chaos of everyday life in a large city."

Bo Newell

Bo Newell's realistic paintings of African wildlife demand attention, while his surreal paintings—his *trompe l'oeil*—command a second, third and fourth look. The latter may not please traditionalists, but they show a marvelous imagination at work, a creativity and technical ability that none can deny. And with each of them, Newell gives himself new challenges. In "No Boundaries," for example, he decided to create not two, but three paintings in one, in order to add depth and movement to the work and to draw the viewer deeper into it. Then he gave each space its own light source—moonlight for the inner painting, a sunset for the book, a candle for the room.

Born in Ponca City, Oklahoma, in 1950, Newell has been "playing" with animals since he was in kinder-garten—when he began creating them from mounds of clay. One of the five-year-old's figures was included in a children's exhibit at the Museum of Fine Arts in Boston. When his family moved to an isolated area of Colorado, the still-young Newell got more serious about his sculpting and created his own miniature jungles. "I would try to find pictures to help me get everything authentic and in proper proportion," he says. "When I was eight years old, my uncle gave me my first oil kit, and soon I was painting oils on canvas."

By the time he was in high school, Newell's family had

"Mayan Transformation" is 48 inches wide by 36 inches high. Newell's "Outward Bound," opposite page, is 30 inches wide by 40 inches high. (Photo of artist: Tommy Barbee; Courtesy of Charlie Sammut, "Wild Things" Game Preserve)

Bo Newell's "No Boundaries" portrays animals coming out of one inner image and stepping into another. The original oil is 48 inches wide by 30 inches high. "Fortitude," opposite page, is 36 inches wide by 48 inches high. "Mystery of the Wolves," right, is 48 inches wide by 36 inches high.

moved to California. There, he studied at the Chouinard Institute in Los Angeles, then went to Texas Tech University, Lubbock, Texas, where he earned a B.F.A. degree in fine art. His mother wanted him to become a doctor, and he began taking pre-med courses, but he hated the math, and the idea of never having time for his art, he says, "made me sick."

Determined to support himself as a wildlife artist, Newell made his first of many trips to Africa in 1974. Although he's been charged by an elephant at Lake Manyara, by a rhino in Crater, and was "almost attacked by lions in Tsavo," he loves the continent and its wildlife. "Africa was at first a place where I escaped, just to use imagination," he explains. "The more interested I became, the more I found out about the reality of the animals and their world." He now works diligently to save the land and its animals, in part through the contribution of paintings to the Safari International Clubs, the Cheetah Conservation Fund and other preservation groups, including Houston Zoological Society. He hopes that his artworks cause others to remember and appreciate the beauty of wildlife and nature. "They are both precious gifts from God to man, and we should do our best to preserve them," he asserts.

While Newell's love of animals is unlimited, he does have favorites to paint. "I love the zebras' stripes," he says. "They are perfect subjects for both realism and sur-

realism. Every zebra has a different pattern, and there are even different patterns on opposite sides of the body of the same zebra. The elephant's size is very impressive. Its sense of presence has intrigued me since childhood," he notes.

Newell, who has been honored as Artist of the Year by both the Houston and the Dallas Safari Clubs, uses oil paint, acrylics, pencil and bronze to depict majestic and near-extinct animals. His originals, many of which are commissioned, sell for $2,500 to $30,000. Prints of his paintings are issued by Archetype Publishing, Los Gatos, California.

Jerry Raedeke

Two early influences helped direct Jerry Raedeke's career. The first was "growing up with a father who had a deep love for the natural world," says the artist, who was born in Madison, South Dakota, in 1941. The second: "During my grade-school years, we lived next to a professional wildlife painter, who let me paint with him in his studio." By the time he was eleven, Raedeke had sold his first painting; he continues to sell his originals, as well as prints of his work, which are published by Hadley House, Bloomington, Minnesota.

Raedeke's childhood paintings were oils, but today he prefers to use transparent watercolors. His paintings are representational—he is "less interested in detail," he explains, "than in conveying the feeling of the scene or subject." His success at this has earned the artist many honors and awards. Raedeke was, for instance, the Southeastern Wildlife Exposition's 1989 Artist of the Year, the 1990 Minnesota Ducks Unlimited Artist of the Year, and the 1993 Kansas Ducks Unlimited Artist of the Year. His artwork was selected for the 1991 Iowa Duck Stamp, the 1993 Kansas Duck Stamp, the 1993 Georgia Duck Stamp and the 1993 Georgia Ducks Unlimited Sponsor print. His work has also been featured in numerous magazines, including *Midwest Art, Minnesota Waterfowler, Wildlife Art News, Artists' Magazine, American Hunter, Turkey Call, The Correspondent* and *The Minnesota Volunteer*. He was featured nationally in a documentary for public television and in the "Prairie Sportsman" series on Minnesota Public Television.

The artist's passion for painting is coupled with a strong interest in religion. Upon graduating from high school, he attended Gustavus Adolphus College, St. Peter, Minnesota, where he studied fine art, but earned a degree in philosophy, graduating with honors in 1963. Several years later, he did graduate work at Concordia Seminary, Springfield, Illinois; he earned a Master of

"Quiet Cove," 26 inches wide by 14 inches high, has been published by Hadley House in a signed and numbered edition of 750. "I especially enjoy watching and painting the large birds," says Jerry Raedeke. "There is a special grace to their flight, and their size invites interesting play of light."

"Those Were the Days" has been published by Hadley House in a limited edition of 500. The signed and numbered print is 14 inches wide by 9⅞ inches high.

Divinity degree in 1968, and was ordained as a Lutheran minister. Between his college graduation and seminary, he lived in Los Angeles and studied with Jake Lee, a well-known Chinese-American watercolorist.

Over the years, Raedeke has spent "many hours in the field for firsthand observation, and countless miles of travel to a great variety of places." Those "places" include 38 of the 50 United States, 6 Canadian provinces and 19 other foreign countries. He has exhibited at almost all the major wildlife shows in this country, but is currently doing just one a year—Charleston's Southeastern Wildlife Exposition. He still enjoys meeting his collectors, though, and is known for remarquing his prints at personal appearances.

The artist hopes that his paintings will evoke "feelings of joy and wonder," that viewers will experience "the great miracles of creation, and hopefully awakenings of commitment and responsibility towards its preservation." His personal commitment to the preservation of wildlife and its habitat takes two forms. Raedeke is a Life Sponsor of Ducks Unlimited, and he has donated more than 150 original paintings and 75,000 prints to the organization. Through the sale of these artworks, Ducks Unlimited has raised more than five million dollars for wetland restoration. Also, the artist works actively in Minnesota—the state he now calls home—on water-quality issues and land-use regulations, as chairman of the Regional Watershed Board of Managers, and with other area environmental concerns.

Gamini Ratnavira

Born in Colombo, Sri Lanka, in 1949, Gamini Ratnavira found sanctuary from boarding school in his country's rain forests. "I would fill all my sketchbooks with the flora and fauna that I observed," he recalls. "I would return with these jewels of nature to share with my schoolmates, and kept at it until they could recognize and experience each species." His keen enjoyment of nature—and of sharing his discovers with others—continues. Australia, Singapore, Zimbabwe, The Maldive Islands, Costa Rica, Mexico, Belize, Peru—these are just a few of the places he's visited in order to observe, photograph and sketch wildlife in its natural habitat. To share his experiences, the artist—who currently lives in Fallbrook, California, with his two children, Neil and Natalie—leads nature tours to Peru, Sri Lanka and Central America. He also teaches school children about wildlife conservation through the Naturalist at Heart program.

Besides lecturing on wildlife and leading tours, Ratnavira helps support a variety of conservation groups, including Sri Lanka's World Wildlife Fund and the Texas Endangered Species Project. He has donated original paintings and prints to many groups, too, including Endangered Carnivores, the Florida Nature Conservancy, Center for Endangered Cats, The San Diego Zoo and Wild Animal Park, the Bermuda Zoo and Aquarium, and Fallbrook Land Conservancy. He is an avid birdwatcher, and boasts a life list of 3,634. In Sri Lanka, he bred tropical birds, reptiles and mammals, "hosting at one time more than 600 birds in my aviary," he says.

Ratnavira attended the DeMazanod College in Sri

"Spirit of Iguazu," depicting a jaguar, is a 48-inch-wide by 24-inch-high oil painting. It's been published as a canvas Giclée, in a limited edition of 50. Featuring keel-billed toucans and a red-eyed tree frog, "Hide and Seek," left, is 30 inches wide by 24 inches high. It has been published in an edition of 250 prints and 50 artist proofs. Gamini Ratnavira's love of animals stems from his youth. "I had a pet orphan Sri Lankan elephant named Maya that filled my childhood days with joy," he says.

Lanka, but is a self-taught artist. He began drawing at age five, filling his school exercise books with sketches "much to my teachers' complaints," he says. He credits his parents for giving him an eye for detail and a flair for design. His father was a jeweler; his mother did exquisite embroidery and hand-crafted silk flowers. The work of other artists, including Claude Monet and wildlife painters such as

"Macaw Talk," a 40-inch-wide by 30-inch-high acrylic, is also available as a print. It was released in an edition of 1,200 prints and 100 artist proofs. "Shadow Dancer," left, depicts a tri-colored heron; it is 30 inches wide by 15 inches high. An oil, it has been published in a canvas-Giclée edition of 50.

John Seerey-Lester, Robert Bateman and Robert Kuhn, have influenced him, but the inspiration for his art comes purely from nature. Ratnavira has a photographic memory that, combined with years of nature study, enables him to paint highly realistic and detailed birds and animals in accurate environments. He uses many media, including oil, acrylic, watercolor and gouache. He also sculpts. His paintings—originals sell for between $400 to $40,000—are reproduced as prints, on stamps and on collector plates.

Ratnavira's eight- by sixteen-foot canvas of Sri Lankan parrots is on display at the Colombo Airport; other Ratnavira canvases are in the collections of the San Diego Natural History Museum, the Endangered Species of Texas museum and the Sri Lankan Natural History Museum. His paintings have been featured in numerous magazines, including Airlanka's in-flight magazine, *Zoonooz*, *Bird Talk*, *Bird World*, *Wildlife Art* and *U.S. Art*. He has illustrated several books, including *Even Frogs Care*, written by his nine-year-old daughter, and *Toucans of the World*, by renowned aviculturalist Dick Schroeder. The artist can be found at about a dozen North American wildlife shows each year; his artwork can be found in galleries around the world.

Terry Redlin

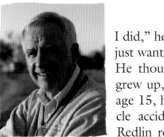

In 1996, Terry Redlin and his wife, Helene, moved back to Watertown, South Dakota, where he was born in 1937. Their home, flanked by a lake and a pond, is surrounded by the wildlife that appears in so much of Redlin's art. It's also near the Redlin Art Center, where more than 100 of Redlin's original oils, along with examples of his commercial art projects and architectural renderings, are on display. Redlin's son, Charles, had the idea for the museum and designed it, while Redlin footed the project's bills of more than $10 million. When completed, he gave the museum to the State of South Dakota as a thank you for having funded his college education. That's just one example of Redlin's philanthropy, though. His donations of art to wildlife conservation groups have raised more than $40 million for their work.

As a youngster, Redlin lived to hunt and fish. "That's all I did," he says. "School was not my bag at all...I just wanted to be outside, hunting and fishing." He thought he'd be a forest ranger when he grew up, but that dream was crushed when, at age 15, he lost a leg as the result of a motorcycle accident. Rather than wallow in self-pity, Redlin reviewed his options. "I wanted to do something outside, but knew long hours or standing or manual labor wasn't in my future. I'd always drawn as a child—it was easy for me—so I thought about going to art school." He was able to do so because the State of South Dakota offered to pay his tuition. "It's why we put the museum here," says the artist, "because this state gave me

"Autumn Shoreline," 24 inches wide by 15¼ inches high, has been published by Hadley House in a signed and numbered edition of 14,500. Porcelain plates and other collectibles featuring Redlin's art are available from The Bradford Exchange, Niles, Illinois.

"The Social Hour," 28⅜ inches wide by 16½ inches high, has that inviting, back-to-nature feeling so prevalent in Redlin's work. "I like to depict the early morning or late evenings, when the shadows are long and warm, and you get that fuzzy feeling that comes after you've been hunting all day," says the artist. "Backwoods Cabin," left, is 24 inches wide by 14 inches high. An Encore Canvas reproduction of it has been issued in an open edition.

that grubstake to go to school, and it would have been virtually impossible otherwise."

After graduating from St. Paul's School of Associated Arts, Redlin worked as a commercial artist and a magazine art director. What he really wanted to do, though, was paint. He reached that goal through a five-year plan that encompassed extensive field work, research, painting, and publishing and selling prints of his art, while holding a full-time job. Because he couldn't afford to advertise his prints, he talked editors into exchanging ad space for magazine-cover illustrations. The result: His prints sold like hotcakes and his cover illustrations gave him national recognition. By 1979, Redlin was able to quit his job and devote his time to painting. Since then, he's received many awards and honors, including having his art featured on the 1981

and 1984 Minnesota Duck Stamps. He was named Ducks Unlimited Artist of the Year in 1983, inducted into the *U.S. Art* Hall of Fame in 1992, and for eight consecutive years, he's been honored as "America's Most Popular Artist" by *U.S. Art*.

Besides wildlife, Redlin paints period pictures of America's small towns and country. "I was the first in my group of wildlife artists to do non-wildlife paintings. The galleries had a fit, until they sold like crazy. 'Coming Home,' that was my first non-wildlife print. It took a week or two for the public to see it, and then they jumped on it. Now all kinds of wildlife artists are painting other things, too," he notes.

Today, Redlin's life centers around promoting the Redlin Art Museum—which opened in June 1997 and has already had more than one million visitors—and tourism in South Dakota. And he still paints. "I'm addicted to it," he says. "I tried quitting, thinking its time to relax and enjoy other things, but there isn't anything that I enjoy as much."

Maynard Reece

I could be a landscape painter. All my sketches done in the field are landscapes. I don't put birds in them," says Maynard Reece, America's preeminent painter of waterfowl and game birds. Early in his impressive career, the octogenarian painted many subjects, including fish, insects, corn, weeds and the wildflowers of Europe; today, however, Reece paints "almost exclusively North American birds. I'm currently working on paintings of turkeys, quail, ducks. I do six to eight major paintings a year, and have commissions that will take me at least another two years to complete."

Born in Arnolds Park, Iowa, in 1920, Reece spent his childhood exploring the lakes and marshes of northern Iowa. During his late teens, he worked at Meredith Publishing Company, in Des Moines, first in the copy department, later as a commercial artist. Then, in 1940, he got a job as assis-

tant curator at the Iowa State Department of History and Archives. Reece credits the late Jack Musgrove—naturalist, author, and past director and curator of the Iowa State Department of History and Archives—with teaching him much of what he knows about birds. He credits another Iowan, conservationist and Pulitzer-prize-winning political cartoonist Jay N. "Ding" Darling, for helping him hone his artistic skills.

In 1950, Reece left the Iowa State Museum of History in order to work full-time as an artist. He did free-lance assignments for *The Saturday Evening Post*, *Sports Illustrated*, *Life* and *Successful Farming*. Meanwhile, he painted waterfowl, but unlike many other wildlife artists at the time, he paid as much attention to the settings in which he placed the birds—his "landscapes"—as he did to the birds themselves. His paintings quickly gained national attention. He won five

Reece's "Misty flight—Canada Geese" is 42 inches wide by 14 inches high.

"Eighty Mallards" is 60 inches wide by 36 inches high. It has been published by Mill Pond Press as a Giclée on canvas, in a limited edition of 80, plus 8 artist proofs. Reece, who has always paid as much attention to his backgrounds as his birds, especially enjoys painting water.

Federal Duck Stamp competitions and two awards from the New York Art Directors' Club. He painted the 1972 First of Iowa State Duck Stamp, was Ducks Unlimited's 1973 Artist of the Year and was honored as Master Wildlife Artist by the Leigh Yawkey Woodson Art Museum at its 1989 "Birds in Art" exhibition.

In the 1990s, Reece created the artwork for four annual Habitat stamps for the Illinois Department of Nature Resources; he also created the artwork for the 1998 Idaho Duck stamp. In 1999 he executed the artwork for the U.S. Seniors Golf Tournament's print—it depicts a golf course, but includes mallards and swans. Two books of his work have been published: *The Waterfowl Art of Maynard Reece* and *The Upland Bird Art of Maynard Reece*. Also, for the past three decades, prints of his work have been published by Mill Pond Press, Venice, Florida.

The honor that has meant the most to Reece came in the late 1990s, when the Iowa Natural Heritage Foundation: The Union Slough National Wildlife Refuge named its 315-acre waterfowl production area for him. Conservation has long been a major concern of the artist, and he has especially strong feelings about our wetlands, which he calls "the most important method of purification of water ever designed."

Maynard and June Reece, his wife of more than fifty years, continue to live in Iowa, as do their two sons. The artist, who has won more Federal Duck Stamp competitions than anyone else, is currently "too busy to even think about entering the contest," but praises its long-term commitment to conservation and the public's support of it.

© Maynard Reece 1993

John A. Ruthven

I believe art is as necessary to our heritage as history books," says John A. Ruthven. "Both record past and present in the effort to educate and enrich the lives of people today and in the future. It is my desire through my paintings to record for later generations some of the beauty of nature that exists in my lifetime."

Born in Cincinnati, Ohio, in 1924, Ruthven has done just that over his long and impressive career. After serving in the Navy during World War II, he attended the Cincinnati Art Academy and Central Academy of Commercial Art. He opened a commercial art studio in 1946, and worked as a commercial artist for the next 17 years. Throughout that time, he painted birds and animals. In 1960, his "Redhead Ducks" painting won the

wonderful artist, but he was a pioneer as well. He was a great recorder of the history of his times. I like to feel I am following in his footsteps," Ruthven says.

Early in his career, Ruthven and a friend, Bill Zimmerman, wrote and illustrated *Top Flight*, a field guide to all the ducks and geese in North America, which contains more than 260 color illustrations. In 1971, he founded Wildlife Internationalé, Inc., which publishes limited-edition lithographs of his paintings. Through this company, the artist works with many wildlife groups; sales of his art have raised millions of dollars for conservation efforts. In 1972, Ruthven was named Ducks Unlimited's First Artist of the Year. He was the First Ohio Duck Stamp Print Artist in 1982, the Trout Unlimited 25th Anniversary Artist of the Year in 1984, the First Ohio Animal Stamp Print Artist in 1988 and Ducks Unlimited's Pacific Flyway Artist in 1989.

Ruthven is a stickler for accuracy, and his research has taken him to Central and South America, Europe, Africa, Asia and the Arctic. One of his most exciting field trips was to the Philippines. Part of a research team from the Cincinnati Museum of Natural History, Ruthven went to the island of Panay in 1989, in search of the Panay striped babbler; a single example of this bird had been discovered two years earlier, and little was known about it. In an article he wrote for the January/February 1991 issue of *Bird Watcher's Digest*, he describes the hardships of that expedition and the excitement of finding a bird that only one other person in recorded history had seen.

In 1994, the Cincinnati Museum of Natural History staged a major retrospective of the artist's work, "John A. Ruthven—In the Audubon Tradition." Many other museums have also featured his work, including the Leigh Yawkey Woodson Art Museum, the Smithsonian Institution, and The Hermitage Museum in Leningrad, Russia (Ruthven's "The Cardinal" is in its permanent collection). One of Ruthven's most cherished memories, though, is of the unveiling of his original "American Bald Eagle" in the White House with President Gerald Ford. "There was a two-hour reception in the East Room in my honor, with more than 200 in attendance," he says.

Ruthven uses a variety of mediums, including watercolor, acrylic, oils and pencil. His originals sell for $2,000 to $75,000 each. Prints of his paintings continued to be published by Wildlife Internationalé, Inc.

"Polish White Eagle" has been published in a limited edition of 300. It is 40 inches wide by 30 inches high. An original acrylic, "Philippine Eagle," opposite page, is 40 inches wide by 50 inches high. This eagle is one of the rarest in the world. In this painting, John A. Ruthven captures it emerging from the pristine forest with a recently captured Rufous Hornbill.

Federal Duck Stamp competition, bringing him national attention. Shortly thereafter, Ruthven gave up his commercial art business, and he's been painting full-time ever since. He is often referred to as the "John James Audubon of the present," and nothing could please him more. "Audubon was my mentor. Not only was he a

Maria A. Ryan

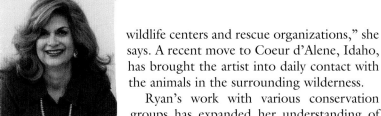

As I was growing up in the country of upper Westchester County, New York, the painting of nature and wildlife seemed to come naturally, starting with portraying my childhood pets and local wildlife," says Maria A. Ryan, who was born in White Plains, New York, in 1942, and began painting at age nine. After graduating from The Graphic Arts Preparatory School of New York, Ryan received formal art training at New York's C.W. Post College. She also has completed 540 workshop hours at Huntington Fine Arts School in New York, and participated in many other workshops in the United States and Europe.

It is, however, Ryan's ability to capture on canvas her love and understanding of wildlife, rather than her well-honed technical abilities, that have made her paintings steady award-winners since 1992. After spending six years in Europe, Ryan settled in Tampa, Florida, and worked as a docent at the Lowry Park Zoo, giving educational tours. She also studied wildlife in its natural habitat. "My travels in the United States have included trips to the Everglades, Olympic, Rocky Mountain, Yellowstone and Grand Teton National Parks, plus many

wildlife centers and rescue organizations," she says. A recent move to Coeur d'Alene, Idaho, has brought the artist into daily contact with the animals in the surrounding wilderness.

Ryan's work with various conservation groups has expanded her understanding of her subjects and provided her with new avenues of expression. For instance, she created the artwork for The Nature Conservancy's narrative signs at the Cougar Bay Preserve in Coeur d'Alene, and she teaches conservation at the preserve to children and adults.

Until recently, Ryan has painted realistic portraits of animals. With the new century, however, the artist began taking an innovative approach to her wildlife art. Creating what she calls "Wildthings," she uses vibrant colors and dynamic, bold strokes to give dimension and character to her subjects. Ryan concentrates on her animals' eyes and expressions, and strives to "tell a charac-

"I enjoy North American wildlife of all types," says Ryan, who is as adept at portraying waterfowl as she is at painting wolves, deer and bobcats. Her "Afternoon Stopover," below, features Canadian geese; limited to an edition of 50 prints on paper, it is 22 inches wide by 14 inches high.

These paintings of wolves show Ryan's change in style. "Time Out," above, is 25 inches wide by 16 inches high; it won First Place at the 1999 Wyoming Western and Wildlife Art Show, held in Casper. Her more recent "Companions," right, is 24 by 24 inches.

teristic story about my subject, sometimes to educate and sometimes to amuse. Through this, I hope to elicit the viewer's interest in and fondness for my subject and for wildlife in general."

In reflecting on her career, Ryan notes, "Someone once said that true success is doing something you really love to do, being good at it, and being recognized for it. I visualize my art career as the superb satisfaction of directing my talents and endeavors toward artistic creation, which I love to do. In this regard, I am most fortunate, since I believe many people are never privileged to feel this way about what they accomplish. I am always creating and learning much in the process through research, studying, artistic techniques and many other facets. My husband is totally supportive in my career, which is invaluable to me. He is my sounding board, my honest broker and critic, my art show partner and advisor. An art career is not a one-person operation, and happily, we work very well together.

"An art career requires an extremely high degree of dedication. I have accumulated a large library and an extensive collection of personally taken photos from which I draw inspiration and information. Workshops, field study trips and seminars broaden my knowledge and develop my abilities. Perhaps most important, the dedication must be there regardless of financial rewards. As any true artist knows, the real rewards emerge from creativity, from learning, from sharing."

Lindsay Scott

"Africa is a place where things change from moment to moment. The same place is never the same, and there's always more than one thing going on at a time," says Lindsay Scott, who knows the continent well. She was born in 1955, in Bulawayo, Zimbabwe (then called Rhodesia), and grew up there, surrounded by the wildlife that populates her paintings. Like the continent, Scott's work is full of movement, often combining animals and birds to give a greater sense of immediacy, of momentary change.

Even as a youngster, Scott was passionate about the birds and animals of Africa. She learned how to survive in the bush, and to be alert to the nuances of the various species. She loved to draw and, taken with Leonardo da Vinci's figure drawings, began honing her own skills at depicting bone structure and muscular systems. Encouraged by a high school art teacher, Scott attended the Michealis School of Fine Art in Cape Town, South Africa. Like too many talented wildlife artists, she experienced her instructors' disdain for realistic art. Abstract art was the order of the day. Undaunted, she studied botany, biology and zoology, while continuing to sketch wildlife. Then she transferred to the University of Minnesota, where she earned a fine art degree; her minor was in biology.

Scott's scientific training and artistic skills were put to use when she got a job as a botanical researcher at the University of Cape Town, and as a curator of paleobotany and ornithology at the South African Museum. She conducted natural history field trips throughout Africa and Antarctica, and spent 14 months in Australia researching and sketching birds for The National Geographic Society.

The artist uses two mediums for her realistic portray-

"Shore Patrol" is a 52-inch-wide by 40-inch-high oil. "The Contenders," opposite page, has been published by Mill Pond Press in a signed and numbered edition of 450. The print is 32½ inches wide by 20¾ inches high. Notice how the the birds in these paintings add to drama and the immediacy of the scenes.

als of animals: graphite and oil paints. It was a drawing of mourning doves that got her into the Leigh Yawkey Woodson Art Museum's 1984 "Birds in Art" exhibition, which brought her to the attention of American collectors; since then, her work has been in ten more of the juried exhibitions. Other honors include a one-woman show at the Santa Barbara Museum of Natural History, and being the 1995 Southeastern Wildlife Exposition's Featured Painter. Scott has received an Award of Excellence from the Society of Animal Artists, and Best of Show and First Place awards at the Pacific Rim Wildlife Show. Her work has been featured in a number of magazines, including *Sporting Classics*, which ran a

cover story on her in its November/December 1995 issue. Prints of her original paintings, which are executed on Belgium portrait linen, are published by Mill Pond Press, Venice, Florida.

Scott moved to California in the mid 1980s, but she returns often to Africa to observe the animals that were so much a part of her youth. While her intimate knowledge of them is important to her art, her paintings bring a fresh perspective to the personalities of the various species; they tell stories, create moods and, the artist hopes, raise the consciousness of those who view them. "I hope that what I do encourages people's desire to learn more and preserve what precious little resources are left...Nature is the most healing thing on this planet. I try to bring a little bit of that indoors," says the artist and ardent conservationist.

John Seerey-Lester

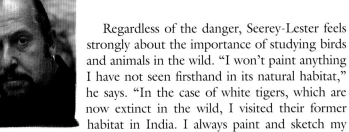

I went to East Africa in 1980 and decided wildlife was what I wanted to paint. Until then," says John Seerey-Lester, "I'd painted many things, mainly nostalgic street scenes and portraits." Since then, the artist has traveled not just throughout Africa, but also to Antarctica, China, India, and South, Central and America. During those travels, he's gotten to know his subjects well. "In Alaska," he says, "I was sketching a grizzly and cub through a scope. She was about 1½ miles away. A cow moose disturbed her grazing on the tundra—she stood, then ran towards me. My camper was about 30 yards to my left. I had to decide whether to stay put or run for the camper—I chose the latter. I got to within six feet of the camper as she and her cub came over the final rise. I froze as she bounded by me. I now have a healthy respect for grizzlies and their speed—approximately 35 miles per hour. It's like a car coming at you!"

Regardless of the danger, Seerey-Lester feels strongly about the importance of studying birds and animals in the wild. "I won't paint anything I have not seen firsthand in its natural habitat," he says. "In the case of white tigers, which are now extinct in the wild, I visited their former habitat in India. I always paint and sketch my subjects from life. I think it is important to learn as much as possible about the animal or bird you are painting—the only way to do this is sketch it from life."

Born in Manchester, England, in 1945, Seerey-Lester grew up with a pencil in his hand. "Instead of watching TV," he says, "I had a pad on my lap and was drawing. My

"The Thinker" portrays a mountain gorilla that Seerey-Lester sketched and photographed in the Impenetrable Forest of Uganda. A canvas reproduction of it was issued in an edition of 350 for Earth Day 2000, as a fund-raiser for the protection of the animal. It is 36 inches wide by 24 inches high.

"Making Tracks," 18 inches wide by 24 inches high, has been published by Hadley House on paper and canvas. The signed and numbered print edition is limited to 999; the canvas edition is limited to 195. "Young Eyes," left, has been published in a signed and numbered edition of 999. It is 10 inches wide by 30 inches high.

parents encouraged me to paint when they realized I had a talent." Another childhood interest that has stayed with him: "Breeding and releasing butterflies—creating butterfly gardens. I have done this since I was 12 years old," he says. After studying graphic design, fashion, textile design, printing, photography and painting at Salford Art College, Seerey-Lester worked in marketing and publishing. He began painting full time in 1974, and moved to the United States eight years later. Prints of his work are published by Hadley House, Bloomington, Minnesota.

Seerey-Lester's art has received many awards, and he was named Master Artist by *U.S. Art* in 1998. Perhaps the honors that mean the most to him, though, are those concerning his conservation efforts, such as his one-man fund-raising show for the World Wildlife Fund for Nature, and his work with Richard Leakey to save the elephant in Kenya. In 1984, he received a commendation from England's Prince Philip for his contributions to wildlife conservation. Another honor: being chosen for Canada's Ducks Unlimited 50th anniversary stamp and print.

About his paintings, Seerey-Lester says, "Composition is vital. My works are contemporary in design, painterly, often impressionistic, but always anatomically correct. Each painting has its own story," he adds. "I always try to create a mood or atmosphere in my paintings. I use light to direct the viewer's eye to the desired location on the painting, or to create the atmosphere I want. The end result, hopefully, is for viewers to feel they come close to what I experienced."

Daniel Smith

As a commercial artist, Daniel Smith illustrated everything from soup to nuts, literally. After studying commercial art at Mankato State University—located in Mankato, Minnesota, where Smith was born in 1954—he got a job in Minneapolis, the heart of America's food industry. There he did ad agency work for General Mills, Betty Crocker, Yopley Yogurt and the like. At nights and on weekends, though, he painted the wildlife that was so much a part of his youth.

Smith's father raised and trained quarter horses; he also had a riding stable and took groups out on trail rides. "I was involved in that when I was a little dude," says the artist. Riding through rural Minnesota, plus hunting and camping with his father, gave Smith an early exposure to wildlife. "I started doing wildlife art when I was in grade school," he says. "Minnesota was a Mecca

for wildlife art at that time, with people like Dave Maass, Les Kouba and Owen Gromme living and working there." Modest about his own talent, Smith didn't even think about pursuing a career as a wildlife painter, but by 1983, the paintings he was doing "for recreation" were in such demand that he was able to abandon his commercial work and paint full-time.

That year, Smith won the first-ever Minnesota Pheasant Stamp competition. Since then, he has created the artwork for more than two dozen other conservation stamps, including the 1988-89 Federal Duck Stamp, Australia's 1989 First of Nation Duck Stamp, the 1991 Minnesota Duck Stamp, the 1991 Texas Waterfowl Stamp, the 1991 National Fish and Wildlife Foundation Stamp, and the United Kingdom's 1991 First of National Duck Stamp. Smith's list of honors is equally impressive and also too lengthy to list. It includes many Best of Show awards, being inducted in the *U.S. Art* magazine's Hall of Fame in 1996, and having his work featured in the Leigh Yawkey Woodson Art Museum's "Birds in Art" exhibition.

In the mid 1990s, Smith, his wife and three children moved from Minnesota to "a really great spot outside of Bozeman, Montana. Elk are around continually, and there are bear, whitetail deer, mule deer, foxes, coyotes, and I expect we'll be seeing wolves in a couple of years," says the artist—a dedicated conservationist who actively supports Yellowstone Wolf Recovery, the International Wolf Center, World Wildlife Fund, Ducks Unlimited and others.

With Yellowstone practically in his backyard, Smith is painting a lot of North American wildlife, but you'll find his signature on paintings of everything from African wildlife to the exotic birds of South America's rain forests. He generally uses acrylics to create highly realistic scenes. Collectors may see a change in his style down the road, though. "I think people are beginning to open up to a looser, more impressionistic kind of depiction, not quite as photo-realistic as my art is, and that's a direction I might take in the future," he says. He also notes that today's collectors appreciate a wider variety of subjects. Still, there will always be a demand for art depicting the old favorites. "That's always a challenge, stepping up to the plate and painting a wolf or an eagle—something that's been done over and over—and painting it in a new, fresh and invigorating way." As collectors of Smith's art know, that's a challenge he has no problem meeting.

"Forever Free," above left, is 37 inches wide by 25 inches high. It has been published on canvas in an edition of 2,500. The setting for this dramatic portrayal of an eagle is Alaska's Kenai River. "Primal Instinct," opposite page, is 24 inches wide by 36 inches high. "I often paint landscapes and use wildlife as the focal point," says Daniel Smith, "but I also paint a fair amount of water." Prints of his paintings are published by Mill Pond Press, Venice, Florida.

Morten E. Solberg

Morten E. Solberg hopes that his paintings portray "how it feels to be in the presence of wildlife, whether it is on the ledge of a mountain studying mountain goats or observing lions at a kill." In order to bring this immediacy to his work, Solberg will travel to wherever his subject may be. Then he observes, photographs and, when time permits, sketches the animal in its environment. This field work can be dangerous, though, as he and other wildlife artists have learned. "When in Africa for the first time," he says, "Bob Kuhn, Guy Coheleach, Lindsay Scott, Paul Bosman, Bob Koenke and I ended up in the middle of an elephant stampede. I had a tusker come within ten feet of me when she stopped, flapped her ears, turned around and left. Very scary," he admits.

Born in Cleveland, Ohio, in 1935, Solberg never wanted to be anything other than an artist. His early interest in art was inspired, in part, by the beauty of tapestries that his paternal grandmother had done as a young woman. Solberg studied at the Cleveland Institute of Art, then worked in various design studios. Eventually, his commercial art work took him to

"Winged Victory" has been published by Hadley House in a signed and numbered edition of 950. The print of Solberg's original watercolor is 29½ inches wide by 21½ inches high. "Arctic Solitude," opposite page, has been published in a limited edition of 999 signed and numbered pieces; it is 29 inches wide by 15 inches high. An avid conservationist who donates to wildlife groups around the world, Solberg hopes his paintings will help others understand what it feels like to be in the presence of wildlife. (Photo of artist: Norman Lightfoot)

California, the state that he and his wife, Terri, call home today. Solberg began painting full-time in 1971; he is a member of the American Watercolor Society, the National Watercolor Society, the Society of Animal Artists, Wildlife Artists of the World and Knickerbocker Artists.

An interest in painting animals began when Solberg was in high school. Over the years, he's depicted many other subjects, including flowers, landscapes, Western themes and Native Americans—one of his great grand-mothers was the daughter of a Mohawk chief. However, what he enjoys painting the most is wildlife, and he is best known for his exquisite renderings of birds and animals in their natural habitats.

Solberg uses a variety of mediums, including water-color, acrylic, gouache and oil. He describes his style as impressionistic, yet the animals in his paintings are quite detailed and realistic. What is of utmost importance to Solberg is mood. "If I cannot create the proper mood for the particular wildlife species, I have not been successful," he says.

Solberg's art has been featured on the covers of a number of magazines, and he and his work have been the subject of numerous articles in magazines such as *American Artist, Wildlife Art News, Art West, Watercolor, Sports Afield, Sporting Classic* and *Grays Sporting Journal*. He is a member of *U.S. Art* magazine's Hall of Fame, and has won many awards for his work. His paintings can be found in the Smithsonian Institution, National Gallery of Art, National Academy of Design, Leigh Yawkey Woodson Art Museum, The Cleveland Museum of Art, The Dunnegan Museum of Art, and in corporate and private collections. His originals command prices of up to $35,000; prints of his paintings are published by Hadley House, of Bloomington, Minnesota.

Robert Steiner

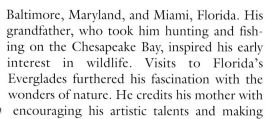

"I am very proud that my work has raised more than three million dollars for wetlands preservation," says Robert Steiner. Often dubbed "the king of duck stamps," the artist celebrated his 52nd state duck stamp in the year 2000. Also to his credit: The 1998-99 Federal Duck Stamp. In addition to holding the record for number of duck stamps featuring his art, Steiner has influenced the style of conservation stamp art. "When I started entering duck stamp competitions, almost all stamp art depicted two ducks on an almost flat background. They were purely graphic—not really paintings at all. I was the first artist to do a winning image with a real complete landscape in the background," Steiner says. This trend-setting painting won the 1984 Nevada Duck Stamp contest; it was one of 314 entries. The painting features a pair of sprig with Nevada's Stillwater in the background.

The artist was born in Philadelphia, Pennsylvania, in 1949, but he spent his youth in Baltimore, Maryland, and Miami, Florida. His grandfather, who took him hunting and fishing on the Chesapeake Bay, inspired his early interest in wildlife. Visits to Florida's Everglades furthered his fascination with the wonders of nature. He credits his mother with encouraging his artistic talents and making sure he got art lessons as a child. "In elementary school the other kids liked my war pictures enough that I was able to make my first sales for baseball cards," he says. At age 18, Steiner won a *National Scholastic* magazine art contest and received a scholarship that enabled him to go to the Rhode Island School of Design, where he earned a B.A. degree. "I studied painting there, but it was pretty much modern art; they didn't teach much in the way of realistic technique, so that was something I had to teach myself," Steiner notes.

After college graduation, Steiner moved to California and sold pen-and-ink drawings to tourists for a few years. Then he enrolled in San Francisco State University and earned an M.A. degree in fine art print making. With this degree in hand, he got part-time teaching jobs and supplemented his income by doing magazine illustrations. "Then I heard about the duck stamp contest, and I thought, 'Oh, this sounds like fun.' The deadline for the first Federal Duck Stamp contest I wanted to enter had already passed by, so I entered the California contest and came in second." That was quite a feat, since his entry was the first painting he'd ever done of a duck! Encouraged, he began studying and painting waterfowl, and the next year, 1981, he

Robert Steiner's "Barrow's Goldeneye," left, won the 65th Federal Duck Stamp Contest and was featured on the 1998-99 federal stamp and print. His artwork for the 1989 New Hampshire Duck Stamp is seen above. Like all federal and state duck stamp paintings and prints, it is 9 inches wide by 6½ inches high.

Steiner enjoys breaking tradition with his duck stamp art. For instance, his 1994 New Mexico Duck Stamp art, above, features a whole flock of birds, rather than the usual pair. His artwork for the 1999 California Duck Stamp art is shown at left. Steiner's first winning duck stamp art graced California's 1981 stamp. The artist works in a "super-tight" style. "I'm pretty obsessive on detail, which is very popular in wildlife art," he says, "but I also try to create strong, dramatic lighting."

Observing waterfowl is now one of Steiner's favorite pastimes, and one he doesn't have to go far to enjoy. "There's quite a bit of waterfowl on the San Francisco Bay, just three blocks from my home. Inland is the Suisun Marsh, which is the world's largest brackish marsh. Then two hours away is the Butte Sink, which is a major watering hole for migrating birds. Some of my favorite experiences in life

won California's Duck Stamp contest. Win after win in state competitions, along with numerous commissions, followed. By 1986, Steiner was painting waterfowl full-time and had his own publishing company, Steiner Prints.

have been out in the marshes, feeling the thrill of seeing flocks of waterfowl. I hope my paintings communicate the sense of awe and wonder that I have at being alive and experiencing the beauty of nature," says Steiner.

Lee Stroncek

y mother was a professional artist, so I was exposed to a wide range of art and related materials, such as books, magazines, museum visits," says Lee Stroncek. The renowned wildlife artist, who was born in Minneapolis, Minnesota, in 1951, had his talent encouraged not only at home, but also by art instructors in grade school and high school. Family hunting and fishing trips exposed him to wildlife at an early age, and sparked a deep interest in "animals, wild and rural landscapes, and natural history in general."

After completing high school, he studied wildlife and fisheries biology at the University of Montana and the University of Alaska. He then went on to complete two years of art instruction at Colorado State University, Ft. Collins. Stroncek, who has been painting full-time since 1980, likes his scenes to "elicit feelings of quietness and solitude. I generally choose to depict candid scenes of nature in a peaceful mood," says the artist, who describes his style as semi-impressionistic. "I prefer to depict wildlife as a complimentary part of the landscape. Subtlety of color and strength of design and form are important to me," he adds, noting that each of his subjects calls for a different approach, depending on the overall mood he wants to create in the work. While Stroncek used acrylics for many of his earlier paintings, his current mediums of choice are oil and watercolor.

Stroncek is an avid fly fisherman, canoeist, cyclist, hiker and skier—all activities, he notes, "that get me into places that can spark ideas for paintings." The artist has spent hours observing wildlife, and his memories of time in the field play an important role in his work. However, he also has an extensive reference library comprising per-

"Nesting Swans and Lifting Fog" is 22 by 22 inches. Lee Stroncek used acrylics for "Nomads of the North," opposite page. The painting is 28 inches wide by 18 inches high.

sonal research photos that he's taken on his outdoor treks and wildlife images that he's clipped from diverse sources. Stroncek features a variety of wildlife in his work, but he particularly enjoys painting moose, grizzly bears, trumpeter swans and deer "because they all live in relatively wild, beautiful habitats. Moose," he adds, "project strength and majesty. Grizzlies represent true wilderness. Swans project purity of grace and form, and deer represent shyness and swiftness."

The artist lives in Bozeman, Montana, with his wife and son. He attends several wildlife shows annually, and his work is available in galleries nationwide. His originals sell for $650 to $4,000 each. Prints of Stroncek's paintings are published by Wild Wings of Lake City, Minnesota. His artworks have been featured in a number of magazines, including *Sports Afield, Field & Stream, Fly Fisherman, Trout, Southwest Art, Wildlife Art News, Sporting Classics, Yankee* and *In-Fisherman*; also, his paintings grace the 1985 and 1988 California Wild Trout Stamp prints. One of his paintings is in the permanent collection of the National Museum of Wildlife Art in Jackson Hole, Wyoming, and his work has been selected for several of Leigh Yawkey Woodson Art Museum's prestigious "Birds in Art" exhibitions.

"I prefer to depict wild-
life as a complementary
part of the landscape,"
says Lee Stroncek, whose
"Wind Swept" is shown
above. An original oil, it
is 36 inches wide by 26
inches high. "Winter
Evening Fox," right, is a
30-inch-wide by 26-inch-
high oil painting. "Loons
and Rainbow, Eagle
Lake," opposite page, is
eleven by eleven inches.

Mark A. Susinno

While working full-time in various laborer-type jobs, I was encouraged by my brother Byron—a fly fisherman—to submit entries to various state trout and duck stamp contests," says Mark A. Susinno. "While I was not a fisherman prior to this time, I really began to take to it about the time I won my first stamp contest, the 1986 Maryland Trout Stamp. My passion for fishing continued to grow, and I continued to enter and win a number of trout and fishing stamp contests." In the 1980s and '90s, his art was chosen for 18 trout, salmon and saltwater fishing stamps; he began the year 2000 with his painting of wild brook trout winning the Pennsylvania Trout/Salmon Stamp contest.

Now a resident of Pennsylvania, Susinno was born in Washington, D.C., in 1957, and began to paint at the age of three. "My mother, Maria, enjoyed a variety of artistic pursuits, including oil painting, pastel drawing, sculpting and working in various craft mediums," he says. "She encouraged my siblings and me to explore working with these mediums from a very early age, and I continued into adulthood." He attended Pratt Institute, Brooklyn, New York, and earned a B.F.A. degree in painting. But after graduating with honors, he found himself unfocused artistically. He did a bit of sculpture, and painted in a variety of styles. When he began painting fish, though, he focused on realism. However, he notes, "I avoid painting with strict photographic accuracy, as I prefer to include more color and often more detail than would

"On the Run—Atlantic Salmon" has been published by Wild Wings in a signed and numbered edition of 950 prints on paper and 95 artist proofs. It is 34 inches wide by 24 inches high. "Flat Out—Tarpon, Needlefish, Trunkfish," opposite page, is an original oil; it is 36 inches wide by 24 inches high.

actually be seen underwater." Another thing he avoids: Creating "restful" paintings. Rather than use strong horizontal and vertical lines, he emphasizes diagonal lines. "When composing the painting, I prefer to arrange shapes in such a manner as to lead the viewer's eye to move around the image," he explains. "When I'm told a painting is calming, I presume I have failed."

The easiest fish for Susinno to paint are those he's caught, as once he gets a fish out of water, he photographs it for anatomical details and colors. He takes underwater photos of the fishes' habitat, including rocks, logs, sub-aquatic vegetation and prey. "Since my paintings nearly always make reference to sport fishing and/or fly fishing, I am generally more successful at depicting a believable scenario when I have fished for the particular species in a particular manner," he adds. The fish he most enjoys painting is the tarpon. "This is a large saltwater species that can be found in the inshore waters of the Florida Keys and throughout the Caribbean. The colors and forms of the tarpon's habitat I find very appealing, for one thing, and the fish itself presents interesting challenges because its flanks are as reflective as mirrors, so they reflect the colors of the fish's surroundings."

In the world of wildlife art, fish paintings don't top the popularity charts. But Susinno has earned a reputation as one of the best sporting artists in the country. He is a member of the Society of Animal Artists, and his paintings have been featured in numerous magazines, including *Field & Stream, Wildlife Art News, Sporting Classics, Sports Afield, Gray's Sporting Journal, Trout* and *Fly Fisherman.* Collector plates featuring his paintings have been issued by The Hamilton Collection. Prints of his work are published by Wild Wings, of Lake City, Minnesota. Concerned about conservation, he is a member of Trout Unlimited, the Chesapeake Bay Foundation and the Coastal Conservation Association. He has donated numerous prints to these and other fishing-related conservation organizations for fund-raising purposes.

Gary Robert Swanson

Like the animals he paints, Gary Robert Swanson seems larger than life. He has an energy, a zest for living, a booming laugh that are impossible to resist. He's an adventurer, a raconteur, a man who has faced great danger and lived to tell about it. From modest beginnings on a South Dakota farm, Swanson has become a top wildlife artist and one of the most traveled. "I first went to Africa back in 1962, when I was 20 years old," he says. "Since then, I've been on more than 40 safaris." He's tracked and photographed animals in Africa and Asia. He's climbed the Rockies, the Cassiar Mountains, the Alaskan Range in his search for subjects. "I've been around this grand planet so much, I've got a hundred home bases," says Swanson, adding: "If one is to interpret correctly and honestly, it is imperative that one live the experience, for without the emotion of the experience, what have you to say on canvas?"

Swanson's passion for wildlife came from his father, who was "a most avid fancier of all wild creatures. In addition to his intense interest in nature, he had a loving ability to instill in his junior admirer a zeal to know, to understand and, most of all, to interpret the love I found in nature." Sadly, when Swanson was 15, his father died, and the family lost their farm. His mother remarried, and they moved to California, where Swanson got a job in a supermarket. Then, at age 17, he began working as a taxidermist. After graduating from high school, he got a job in Seattle, and later was transferred to Alaska, but he left there after about a year to open Swanson's Taxidermy with one of his older brothers, Ray, a accomplished painter. Swanson's career as a taxidermist spanned a dozen years, during which he

On his many trips to Africa, Gary Swanson has gained a deep understanding of big cats such as depicted in "Cheetah Family," below. It is 70 inches wide by 38 inches high. "Where Eagles Soar," opposite page, top, is 48 inches wide by 30 inches high. "The Signal Corps," opposite page, bottom, is 44 inches wide by 30 inches high. Notice how these paintings entice you into the scene.

worked for the San Bernadino County Museum and the Los Angeles County Museum.

"I was far too poor to go to college, so I learned from life as I grew," says Swanson. One of the things he learned while working as a taxidermist was how to create interesting backgrounds for the museum exhibits of wildlife. Seeing the quality of his background sketches, his brother Ray encouraged him to paint. Ray taught him technique, and how to mix and use color. Studying the Old Masters taught him about value and intensity. Swanson's innate abilities and drive to succeed did the rest.

"I interpret exactly what I see and, most important, what I feel—that can be anything from love to stark fear and all the prides in between," says Swanson. "If it has four legs and lives wild, it has a story to tell. My job is to figure out that story and tell it true." His success at interpreting those stories has made him an award-winning artist, whose originals go for as much as $250,000 each. Limited-edition prints of his paintings are published by Blackhawk Editions, Danville, California.

Swanson feels an obligation to paint animals and their habitat so if they disappear, there will be a record of the way things were. However, he also works diligently for the preservation of the bongo, the kudu, the big cats, the longhorn sheep and the other animals he so loves. The Audubon Society, Safari Club, Rocky Mountain Elk Foundation and Foundation for North American Wild Sheep are some of the groups he supports. His donated artworks have raised more than one million dollars for conservation efforts around the world.

Gary Robert Swanson's "The Peace Makers," above, is an original oil on linen. It is 50 inches wide by 30 inches high. His "Theodore Roosevelt at the Elk Horn," left, is 44 inches wide by 30 inches high.

Trevor Swanson

"Art is a family business, it seems, and with the kind of influence I had growing up, it was hard *not* to be interested in art," says Trevor V. Swanson—the son of wildlife artist Gary Swanson, and the nephew of Native American artist Ray Swanson. His sister, Kimberly, and a cousin, Mark Swanson, are also painters. With all these artists about, young Trevor's talent was quickly recognized, but he was allowed to develop his artistic abilities at his own speed. "Dad was there, and was always willing to answer my questions, but he never pushed. When I asked for training, however, he taught me all the basics—technique and tricks he'd picked up over the years—and then he let me go. He said that painting is a personal process that I'd have to develop on my own."

An original oil on canvas, "In the Hunt," above, is 40 inches wide and 25 inches high. The 8⅛-inch plate is part of Swanson's African Wildlife Collection from Islandia International. "High Country Griz," opposite page, is 24 inches wide by 30 inches high. It has been published by Blackhawk Editions on paper and canvas. The print-on-paper edition is limited to 500; the canvas edition is limited to 750.

Gary Swanson also taught his son to enjoy nature. "Dad traveled all over the world when we were tiny, and we went with him. I think I was just five when I first went to Africa." At home, too, the family's activities centered around the outdoors and wildlife. "My affinity for animals stems from my childhood, but as I've grown, I've come to appreciate even more how special the creatures of this world are," says the artist, who brings that passion to his paintings. "I like to spend as much time as possible in the field. I try to capture the true 'feel' of the outdoors in my work, so I also spend a lot of time just looking at scenery. All of this means I have the wonderful opportu-nity to travel, hike and spend time doing things I love, and calling it 'work.'"

Swanson was born in Redlands, California, in 1968. He attended Arizona State University, in Phoenix, where he met his wife, Jennifer. When she transferred to the University of Arizona's law school, Swanson accompanied her to Tucson, and began taking education courses at the university. But he quickly realized that he enjoyed painting more than anything else. "About that time," he says, "my paintings began to really sell, so I quit college to paint full-time." Today, his originals sell for $1,000 to $20,000 each. Prints of his work are published by Blackhawk Editions, Danville, California; his paintings appear on plates from Islandia International, Islandia, New York. He was honored as the 1994 Artist of the Year by The Foundation for North American Wild Sheep' 1994 Artist of the Year, and he received the International Collectible Esposition's 1998 and 1999 Best Plate and Best Wildlife Artist awards. He works with Safari Club International, The Foundation for North American Wild Sheep and other groups, helping to raise money for wildlife causes around the world. He hopes his art helps others "feel the beauty and awe of our incredible world."

Swanson and his wife, an attorney, have a young son and daughter, both of whom are beginning to exhibit signs of their famous family's talent. They live in Arizona.

Linda Thompson

The manatees in Florida are just one of the saddest things. There are so few of them, and there's so little being done to try to save them. They're one of the first animals that I painted after moving here, and I issued a limited-edition print of that painting to try to raise awareness of their plight," says Linda Thompson, who has lived in Sarasota, Florida, since she was 23. "Manatees are just one of the subjects that I paint today, but it was my print of them that threw me into the limited-edition print market." Today, Mill Pond Press, of Venice, Florida, publishes prints of her work.

"Gentle Giants (Manatees)" is 40 inches wide by 30 inches high. "Cool Water (Dolphin)," opposite page, is an acrylic on canvas; it is 30 inches wide by 40 inches high.

Born in Canton, Ohio, in 1948, Thompson has had no formal art training, but her innate talent landed her a commercial artist's job with an advertising agency upon her high school graduation. In Florida, she continued to work as a commercial artist. "I was an art director for a magazine, and did a lot of free-lance illustrations. I also did logo designs," she says. Throughout this time, she also painted.

"I've been painting since I was a little kid. I did a lot of commissions for people who had horses—I painted a lot of horses and dogs. I could never warm up to painting people's portraits or landscapes, but put an animal in front of me, and I could do it right away," she says.

Since she began painting full-time in 1986, Thompson has specialized in sea mammals. "I feel that in order to do anything right, you need to really focus on it and study it. I could study everything a little, or I could study marine life a lot, specifically marine mammals." The more she learned, the more ideas she had for paintings, especially paintings of things few people get to see, such as "how dolphins look under water, and turtles and coral reefs and all the different mammals that live in the ocean. I decided to focus my art on what I knew and what I could see right here in Florida. Since then, most of my paintings depict marine mammals and things having to do with water."

Thompson enjoys snorkeling, but notes that in Florida, you don't have to get wet to observe ocean life. "One of my favorite places is Sea World, where you can watch the dolphins under the water," she says. "I can stand there for hours just watching them, taking photos of them. There are penguins there, too. I got my idea for 'Follow the Leader,' a recent print from Mill Pond Press, at Sea World. I was allowed to go into the penguins' compound. I got to photograph them up close, do some sketches, and I got to hold one. It was a great opportunity to see an animal I'd otherwise have to travel to Antarctica to see."

The animals in Thompson's paintings are realistic because, she says, "I like things to look exactly like they are. I want a manatee or a dolphin to look exactly like it does. I'm a little freer with my backgrounds, though; since water is so fluid, I can be artistic in order to give the impression of something flowing or moving. My paintings come from my heart," she adds. "Some of them evoke mystery, but I think they create happy places to think about—good places to go to be relaxed, to think that maybe everything will be okay."

Linda Thompson © 1996

Linda Thompson's "Follow the Leader" is
48 inches wide by 24 inches high.

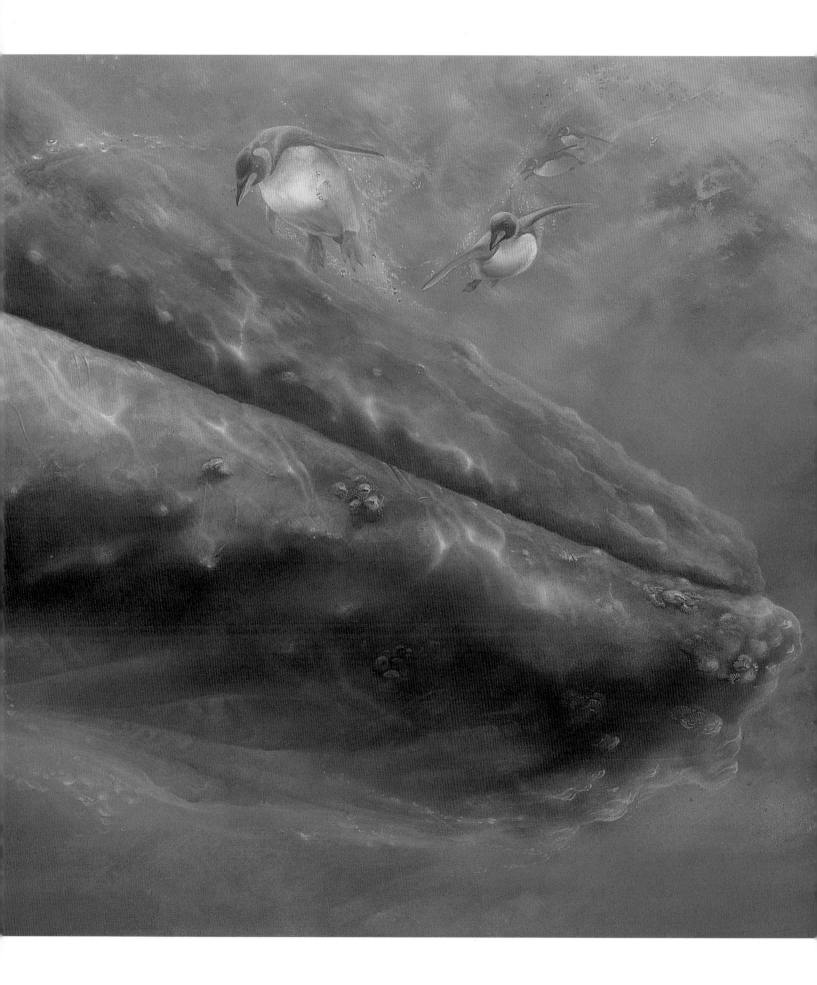

Persis Clayton Weirs

An early exposure to art and a childhood spent outdoors seem to be key ingredients in the making of a wildlife artist. Take, for instance, Persis Clayton Weirs. Her uncle was a portrait artist, whose studio and paintings were "magical" to her as a child. Also, she was fascinated by animals, and there were an abundance of them on Deer Island, Maine, where she was born in 1942. "My sisters and I grew up spending our summers and weekends looking for turtles, frogs and snakes. Glimpses of deer, raccoons and birds were always a treat, too."

As a child, Weirs would draw the wildlife she and her sisters observed in their play. By the time she was 23, she was seriously painting horses. As she sharpened her skills over the next 12 years, she received many commissions to paint portraits of champion show and race horses, and illustrated two books on Paso Fino horses. Then, in the early 1980s, she returned to depicting the wildlife that was so much a part of her early years. She continues to paint horses, but mostly wild ones. For research, Weirs photographs and observes birds and animals in captivity as well as in the wild, studying their habits and behavior. She also studies books and videos for comparison. Then, using either

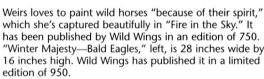

Weirs loves to paint wild horses "because of their spirit," which she's captured beautifully in "Fire in the Sky." It has been published by Wild Wings in an edition of 750. "Winter Majesty—Bald Eagles," left, is 28 inches wide by 16 inches high. Wild Wings has published it in a limited edition of 950.

acrylics or oils, she begins to paint.

"When I'm painting an animal, it's because I find it fascinating and/or beautiful, but I like to include something in the painting that depicts the tension of predator-prey relationships, or loyalty, or humor—something illustrating a natural personality or behavior," says Weirs, who knows that if you watch birds and animals long enough, you'll discover amazing aspects of their lives. For example, she says, "Once I watched an eagle bathing in our beaver pond for about 20 minutes. The eagle totally soaked its wings, and then had difficulty taking off. Flying through my backyard, it couldn't get high enough to clear the trees, so it tried to land in an oak tree. The branch broke, so the eagle grabbed another and wound up hanging upside down, dripping wet and unhappy. It righted itself and eventually flew to another tree, where it spread its wings to dry out. I think of eagles as majestic and noble, but an

upside-down, soggy eagle kind of destroys the image."

In discussing her art—which has been featured at numerous wildlife art shows, including the Leigh Yawkey Woodson Museum's "Birds In Art" exhibition—Weirs says, "I feel eternally puzzled as to why I have been blessed with both this gift and a life that has allowed me to develop my skills to this point. I get to spend my days studying and painting nature's wonderful array of creatures. I feel as though I'm paying tribute to each animal or bird I paint, and I hope that whoever sees the art will recognize the tribute, and see how much I respect and care about the animals."

The artist, who won her home state's 1992 Duck Stamp competition, still lives in Maine, surrounded by wildlife. "There are deer, eagles, osprey, otters, grouse and coyotes right outside our door," she says. "My family and I also live with three horses, two ponies, two sheep, seven cats, one dog, a parakeet and an old disabled crow I've had for 15 years. My crow wakes up every morning excited about everything he can see around him—15 years in a cage and two broken wings haven't dimmed his spirit. He's my inspiration."

Derek C. Wicks

The gift of a animation art kit triggered six-year-old Derek C. Wicks' interest in art. Soon he was drawing and painting pictures of the animals he saw in his grandparents' copies of *National Geographic* magazines. His childhood goal, the Toronto-born-and-bred artist says with a laugh, was to win the *Toronto Sun*'s children's art contest. The prize was having your artwork featured on the newspaper's Sunday TV guide. He attained that goal in 1978, winning the contest at the age of nine.

Wicks artistic talent was encouraged by his parents, and after taking all the art courses he could in school, he entered Sheridan College of Applied Art, Oakville, Ontario. "This is the number one college in North America for animation art and illustration," says Wicks, who studied technical and scientific illustration there, graduating at the top of his class. After earning his diploma, he did free-lance illustration work, mostly for architectural firms, while spending all of his free time painting animals and attending wildlife art shows. "I have always loved animals, and sim-

"Rainman—Mountain Gorilla" is 48 inches wide by 24 inches high. It has been published on canvas in a signed and numbered edition of 50. "Winter Procession—Timber Wolves," opposite page, is 30 inches wide by 20 inches high and has been published on canvas in a limited edition of 150.

ply could not be any other kind of artist," he asserts. "I'm also a big fan of the outdoors and travel. I'll get my dog and head out to the woods on the drop of a dime."

By 1995, Wicks was able to quit taking free-lance jobs and devote all of his energies to his wildlife art, and to traveling the Americas and Africa in search of subjects. "I'll paint anything I've seen that strikes my fancy, from wolves and lions to lemurs and lizards. My favorite animal to depict, though, is the mountain gorilla. Since I was young I have loved the power and grace of these gentle giants. They're the most majestic animal in the world." While there aren't any mountain gorillas in Canada, Wicks says, "Here in Toronto, we have a very famous group of low-land gorillas, which are very close to mountain gorillas in appearance—the low-lands have less of a protruding brow and less hair; as an artist, it is easy for me to 'convert' them into mountain gorillas." Still, Wicks doesn't care to paint animals that he hasn't seen in their natural environment. "My paintings are from personal experience," he

says, adding that "the setting for a painting is as important as the animal itself." In addition to field work, Wicks turns to his "vast collection of photographs, magazines and books on animals" when researching his subjects.

Wicks uses acrylics to create his highly detailed, realistic paintings of animals. "I hope my art gives people a sense of being in the picture," he says, "that they feel like they are interacting with nature—looking through a window into the animal's world." His originals sell for $800 to $18,000 each; prints of his work are available from his company, Wild Realms Publishing. Heralded as one of Canada's most promising young artists, Wicks created the artwork for the 1998 Alberta Conservation Stamp. This means a lot to him, as he is a concerned conservationist and supports the efforts of the Canadian Conservation Fund and the Ontario Human Society Fund. He can be found at some ten wildlife shows annually, and his work can be found in galleries throughout North America.

D. Arthur Wilson

I f I am remembered as having been part of this era of environmental art, I would like it to be not for painting what an animal looked like, or where it lived, or what it ate. Instead, I would like to be remembered as the artist who represented how the animal felt and how he related to you and me," says D. Arthur Wilson. To get to know the animals he paints, Wilson spends extensive time in the field, sometimes just observing wildlife, and at other times, photographing it. He also visits zoos and wildlife compounds, and has an impressive library of reference materials.

tic expression, and he turned to the wildlife that had fascinated him as a youth. He switched to pastels, and developed a distinctive, personal style that he calls "relational art. I like to evoke many emotions with my paintings, including humor," Wilson says. "The wildlife is the vehicle through which I choose to share many human and spiritual truths." The artist paints a variety of animals, but admits to a preference for the large cats. "They're in charge, cunning, and full of color and character," he says. "I also like to depict ostriches in a variety of ways, mostly reflecting peculiar human characteristics."

Wilson's involvement in fund-raising projects for The Digit Fund, The Henry Doorley Zoo, The Okenos Organization, Cheyenne Mountain Zoo and The Denver Zoo have brought him national acclaim. He has also helped raise funds for The Cheetah Conservation Fund. His work with some of these organizations has provided opportunities for him to play with many of the wild animals in his paintings. These experiences enhance his understanding of his subjects, but as he has discovered, they can also be hazardous. "When working with the mission wolf in Silvercliff, Colorado, a young male wolf leaped up and nipped me in my nose—not *on* my nose, *in it*. Wow, the tears automatically started to flow. I have never felt anything like it," he says.

The artist has had more than a dozen one-man shows in the United States, and has had his work featured in

Many of D. Arthur Wilson's works are close-up views of animals' faces, such as this one. Titled "Pensive Passion," it is 30 inches wide by 20 inches high. "Aloft and Aloof," opposite page," is 20 inches wide by 30 inches high. Both have been issued as signed and numbered Giclées, limited to editions of 250.

Born in Brookville, Ohio, in 1958, Wilson was the son of an artist and avid outdoors enthusiast, who shared his love for art and nature with Wilson. "We used to visit Gaitlinburg, Tennessee, and when I saw all the artists on the sidewalk, I was hooked," says Wilson. Although he is self-taught, by the time he was 20, Wilson was supporting himself as a quick-sketch artist. After eight years and more than 4,000 portraits, Wilson wanted to paint something that would give him wider opportunities for artis-

many others. He has been honored with Old Town Tempe Art Exhibition's 1988, '90 and '94 Best of Show awards; Beavercreek Fine Art Exhibition's 1990 Best of Show award; Bolder Creek Art Exhibition's 1992, '94 and '95 Best of Show awards; and Vale Fine Arts Exhibition's 1994 Best of Show award. His originals sell for $650 to $15,000 each. Prints of his work are available from Passion Publishing, Los Gatos, California.

When he's not painting, Wilson loves to travel, scuba dive and hike. "I camp a great deal. I also love to build. When I get a little burned out, I will build a deck, add a bedroom or a hot-tub room to my home. This does as much as anything to refresh me," he says, adding, "Living life to its fullest keeps my work fresh."

Patti Wilson

A dear friend I call my Aunt Barbara, even though she is not my aunt, painted," says Patti Wilson. "Her walls were full of oil paintings, and I loved them. Every time I went to see her, I always would say, 'One day I am going to learn to paint.'" When it came time for college, though, Wilson, who was born in Bakersfield, California, in 1946, chose to major in accounting. Still, she didn't forget that childhood dream, and about 1980, she began to paint as a hobby. "I wanted to fill my house with original oil paintings, but was not in a position to purchase them. So I decided to paint them myself. I began with a still life, which I still love to paint, but when I painted the eyes of my first animal, I got hooked on wildlife," she says.

Several years later, she saw an ad for one of John Seerey-Lester's juried workshops. "At that time, he was only accepting five students per class," Wilson says. "I sent some slides of my work to him and luckily got accepted." On the last evening of the class, Seerey-Lester asked Wilson if she'd ever considered selling her paintings. "I told him I'd never really thought about it and would not even know where to begin. Shortly after the workshop, he called and asked if I would like to exhibit in his students' booth at the Third Annual Orlando Show." Wilson took advantage of that opportunity, and the popularity of her work at that show led to many other exhibits. "The more I exhibited my art, the more I wanted to learn and improve. This is my goal—to keep improving my work," she says. "Being selected the Artist of the Year for the California Wildlife 2000 Open was something I never dreamed would happen to me. What an honor," exclaims Wilson, though she is not entirely new to honors. Her paintings have won a number of awards, including the First Place Art Competition award at the California Open Wildlife Festival 1999.

Wilson is basically a self-taught artist, but she is quick to credit the help she's gotten from studying with other

"Nuzzling," above, is 20 inches wide by 16 inches high. "Sneak Attack," left, is 16 inches wide by 12 inches high; it has been published as a Giclée on watercolor paper. Wilson especially enjoys painting the "little creatures and birds" found near her home.

Patti Wilson's "Down on the Lake" is 16 inches wide by 12 inches high. A Giclée on watercolor paper, it is limited to an edition of 250. Wilson's "Up For the Night," left, is 20 inches wide by 16 inches high.

Wilson especially enjoys painting "little creatures and birds, probably because I have a lot of them around where I live." However, she paints a variety of subjects, including African wildlife, still lifes and portraits. To research her wildlife subjects, she goes hiking and for long walks with her sketchbook and camera in hand. "I also travel to national wildlife

artists. In addition to John Seerey-Lester, she has trained under Gamini Ratnavira, Lee Kromschroeder, Rilla Underwood and Winnie DeSchutter. Wilson describes her style as "super realistic," which she achieves through the use of oils on canvas. Giclée prints of some of her paintings are available from her studio.

preserves, wildlife refuges and national parks," she says. Once back in her studio, using her sketches and photographs as reference, she strives to "create an image that will make the viewer feel like he or she can reach into the painting and touch the animal, and gain an appreciation for the beauty of wildlife."

How to Contact The Artists

Al Agnew
The Al Agnew Collection
11779 Highway 32
Ste. Genevieve, MO 63670

John Banovich
c/o Mill Pond Press
310 Center Court
Venice, FL 34292

Robert Bateman
c/o Mill Pond Press
310 Center Court
Venice, FL 34292

Greg Beecham
c/o The Greenwich Workshop
1 Greenwich Place
Shelton, CT 06484

Ted Blaylock
1152 E. 8th Place
Mesa, AZ 85203

Collin Bogle
14612 NE 80th Place
Redmond, WA 98052

Carl Brenders
c/o Mill Pond Press
310 Center Court
Venice, FL 34292

Carel Pieter Brest van Kempen
c/o Mill Pond Press
310 Center Court
Venice, FL 34292

Darrell Bush
c/o Hadley House
11300 Hampshire Ave. S.
Bloomington, MN 55438

Lee Cable
PO Box 728
Divide, CO 80814

Guy Coheleach
c/o Mill Pond Press
310 Center Court
Venice, FL 34292

Simon Combes
c/o The Greenwich Workshop
1 Greenwich Place
Shelton, CT 06484

Chris Cummings
c/o Wild Wings
2101 South Highway 61
Lake City, MN 55041

Robert Deurloo
PO Box 11
Salmon, ID 83467

Les Didier
c/o Hadley House
11300 Hampshire Ave. S.
Bloomington, MN 55438

Adele Earnshaw
PO Box 1666
Sedona, AZ 86339

Jim Eppler
PO Box 93428
Lubbock, TX 79493

Lindsey Foggett
c/o Hadley House
11300 Hampshire Ave. S.
Bloomington, MN 55438

Eric Forlee
1806 Rushmore Lane
Davis, CA 95616

Rod Frederick
c/o Mill Pond Press
310 Center Court
Venice, FL 34292

Joe Garcia
PO Box 2314
Julian, CA 92036

Nancy Glazier
c/o Somerset House
Publishing
10688 Haddington
Houston, TX 77043

Adam Grimm
7111 N. Murray Ridge Rd.
Elyria, OH 44035

Donald Heywood
Uitspan, 5 Bellevue Ave.
Constantia, Capetown 7806
South Africa

Matthew Hillier
c/o Mill Pond Press
310 Center Court
Venice, FL 34292

Mark Hopkins
Mark Hopkins Sculpture, Inc.
21 Shorter Industrial Blvd.
Rome, GA 30165

Nancy Howe
Triple Jump Studio
RR 1, Box 402
East Dorset, VT 05253
or
c/o Hadley House
11300 Hampshire Ave. S.
Bloomington, MN 55438

Terry Isaac
c/o Mill Pond Press
310 Center Court
Venice, FL 34292

Stephen Koury
Koury Fine Art Gallery
1029 Rustic Estates Dr.
Lakeland, FL 33811

Lee Kromschroeder
1375 Borden Rd.
Escondido, CA 92026
or
c/o Wild Wings
2101 South Highway 61
Lake City, MN 55041

Art LaMay
142 Island Estates Pky.
Palm Coast, FL 32137

Jim Lamb
1604 217th Pl. S.E.
Sammamish, WA 98029

Mark Everett Larson
c/o Pacific Crest Gallery &
Studio
303 Historic E. Columbia River
Hwy.
Troutdale, OR 97060

David A. Maass
c/o Wild Wings
2101 South Hwy. 61
Lake City, MN 55041

Tom Mansanarez
c/o Cattle Creek Publishing
1043 E. 1900 N.
N. Logan, UT 84341

Carl McCleskey
2000 Nightingale Rd.
Cloudland, GA 30731

Bruce Miller
c/o Hadley House
11300 Hampshire Ave. S.
Bloomington, MN 55438

John Mullane
c/o Mill Pond Press
310 Center Court
Venice, FL 34292

Roy Benjiman Nauffts
65 Rosepac Ave.
Brampton, Ontario
Canada L6Z 2R3

Bo Newell
4114 Milton St.
Houston, TX 77005
or
c/o Archetype Publishing
105 N. Santa Cruz Ave.
Los Gatos, CA 95030

Jerry Raedeke
c/o Hadley House
11300 Hampshire Ave. S.
Bloomington, MN 55438

Gamini Ratnavira
Hidden Forest Art Gallery
936 S. Live Oak Park Rd.
Fallbrook, CA 92028

Terry Redlin
c/o Hadley House
11300 Hampshire Ave. S.
Bloomington, MN 55438

Maynard Reece
c/o Mill Pond Press
310 Center Court
Venice, FL 34292

John A. Ruthven
Wildlife Inernationalé, Inc.
202 E. Grant Ave./PO Box 59
Georgetown, OH 45121

Maria A. Ryan
Deer Path Fine Art
4977 Deer Path Trail
Coeur d'Alene, ID 83814

Lindsay Scott
c/o Mill Pond Press
310 Center Court
Venice, FL 34292

John Seerey-Lester
c/o Hadley House
11300 Hampshire Ave. S.
Bloomington, MN 55438

Daniel Smith
c/o Mill Pond Press
310 Center Court
Venice, FL 34292

Morten E. Solberg
621 Edgewater Ave.
Oceanside, CA 92057

Robert Steiner
Steiner Prints
315 Cornwall
San Francisco, CA 94118

Lee Stroncek
818 South Black Ave.
Bozeman, MT 59715
or
c/o Wild Wings
2101 South Highway 61
Lake City, MN 55041

Mark A. Susinno
c/o Wild Wings
2101 South Highway 61
Lake City, MN 55041

Gary Robert Swanson
4617 E. Marconi Ave.
Phoenix, AZ 85032

Trevor V. Swanson
Blackhawk Editions
1092 Eagles Nest Pl.
Danville, CA 94506

Linda Thompson
c/o Mill Pond Press
310 Center Court
Venice, FL 34292

Persis Clayton Weirs
c/o Wild Wings
2101 South Highway 61
Lake City, MN 55041

Derek C. Wicks
Wild Realms Publishing
c/o Shaban Serra Ltd.
12 Clairtrell Dr.
Willowdale, Ontario
M2N 5J6 Canada

Arthur D. Wilson
c/o Passion Publishing
15520 Corinne Dr.
Los Gotos, CA 95032

Patti Wilson
Wilson CM and Publishing
5857 Riggs Court
Bakersfield, CA 93306

About the Author

Joan Muyskens Pursley, a graduate of the University of Iowa's School of Journalism, has spent more than 25 years as a magazine editor and writer, working for The Iowa State Department of History and Archives; Times Mirror Magazines; Family Media; Scott Publications and Collector Communications Corporation, where she is the editorial director and associate publisher of the company's three magazines. She has served as editor of *The Annals of Iowa*; *Miniature Collector*; *Dollmaking–Projects and Plans*; *Dolls*, *Figurines & Collectibles* and *Collector Editions*. She is the co-author (with Karen Bischoff) of *The World's Most Beautiful Dolls*, and is currently at work on a new volume of that book, to be published by Portfolio Press.

Her love of wildlife art and her deep respect for the many wildlife artists she's met over the years inspired this book. She hopes it, in turn, will enhance others' appreciation for artworks that capture the beauty and mystery of animals.